UNDERSTANDING
THOMAS PYNCHON

Pacific
WITHDRAWN
University

Understanding Contemporary American Literature

Matthew J. Bruccoli, *Editor*

PACIFIC UNIVERSITY LIBRARY
FOREST GROVE, OREGON

PS
3566
.Y55
Z74
1986

UNDERSTANDING
Thomas
Pynchon

BY ROBERT D. NEWMAN

UNIVERSITY OF SOUTH CAROLINA PRESS

Copyright © University of South Carolina 1986

Published in Columbia, South Carolina, by the
University of South Carolina Press

Manufactured in the United States of America

Library of Congress Cataloging-in-Publication Data

Newman, Robert D., 1951–
    Understanding Thomas Pynchon.

    (Understanding contemporary American literature)
    Bibliography: p. [139]–146.
    Includes index.
    1. Pynchon, Thomas—Criticism and interpretation.
I. Title.   II. Series.
PS3566.Y55Z74   1986   813′.54   86–7113
ISBN 0–87249–485–3
ISBN 0–87249–486–1 (pbk.)

CONTENTS

EDITOR'S PREFACE

Understanding Contemporary American Literature has been planned as a series of guides or companions for students as well as good nonacademic readers. The editor and publisher perceive a need for these volumes because much of the influential contemporary literature makes special demands. Uninitiated readers encounter difficulty in approaching works that depart from the traditional forms and techniques of prose and poetry. Literature relies on conventions, but the conventions keep evolving; new writers form their own conventions—which in time may become familiar. Put simply, *UCAL* provides instruction in how to read certain contemporary writers—identifying and explicating their material, themes, use of language, point of view, structures, symbolism, and responses to experience.

The word *understanding* in the series title was deliberately chosen. Many willing readers lack an adequate understanding of how contemporary literature works; that is, what the author is attempting to express and the means by which it is conveyed. Although the criticism and analysis in the series have been aimed at a level of general accessibility, these introductory volumes are meant to be applied in con-

EDITOR'S PREFACE

junction with the works they cover. Thus they do not provide a substitute for the works and authors they introduce, but rather prepare the reader for more profitable literary experiences.

M. J. B.

ACKNOWLEDGMENTS

I would like to thank those who contributed to the preparation of this book. Scott Donaldson of The College of William and Mary kindly recommended me for this project. William Harmon and Jack Raper of The University of North Carolina read an earlier version of the chapter on *V.* and offered several helpful comments. David Rosenwasser of Muhlenberg College gave me the benefit of his excellent teaching notes on *The Crying of Lot 49* and argued enthusiastically with me concerning Pynchon. Stephen Yarbrough of Texas A & M University diligently read much of the manuscript and offered many sound editorial suggestions. Ellen McDaniel and Bob Young of Texas A & M University patiently guided me through the quirks of computers and aided me in preparing the final draft of the manuscript. My thanks also to the College of Liberal Arts of Texas A & M University for a research grant during the summer of 1985 that gave me the time to complete a large portion of the book. Finally, I want to express my gratitude to my wife, Vicky, for her love and support. She understands.

UNDERSTANDING
THOMAS PYNCHON

CHAPTER ONE

Pynchon: The Author as Luddite

Career

Thomas Ruggles Pynchon, Jr., was born on May 8, 1937, in Glen Cove, Long Island. His family ancestry can be traced back to the eleventh century, and also figures prominently in New England history. William Pynchon, who serves as the model for William Slothrop in *Gravity's Rainbow*, came to the New World in 1630 and was treasurer of the Massachusetts Bay Colony as well as a founder of Roxbury and Springfield. In the most complete biographical piece on Pynchon to date, Mathew Winston discovered that William Pynchon wrote theological tracts that ran counter to orthodox Calvinism. According to Winston, *The Meritorious Price of Our Redemption*, written in 1650, asserts "that Christ saved mankind through his perfect obedience to God, not through bearing Adam's curse, and 'that Christ did not suffer for us those unutterable torments of Gods wrath, that commonly are called Hell-torments, to redeem our soules from them.' "[1] Pynchon's vigorous anti-Calvinism evidently runs in the family blood.

The family name also occupies an important place in American literature. Nathaniel Hawthorne's *The House of the Seven Gables*, published in 1851, relates the blemished history of the Pyncheon family. Unaware of existing Pynchons, Hawthorne, was unprepared for the two letters of protest that he received from family members who objected to his novel for soiling the family name. One of these letters was from the Rev. Thomas Ruggles Pynchon, a chemistry, geology, zoology, and theology professor and future president of Trinity College, Hartford. His grand-nephew and namesake became the father of the novelist.

Pynchon graduated from Oyster Bay High School, Long Island, New York, as class salutatorian at the age of sixteen in 1953 and won a scholarship to Cornell University, where he matriculated in 1953 in engineering physics. The freshman register for his class contains no photograph of him, foreshadowing his obsession with anonymity. He joined the navy after his sophomore year and returned to Cornell in 1957, taking his B.A. in English in 1959. During his last two years at Cornell he took a course with Vladimir Nabokov and was on the editorial staff of the undergraduate literary magazine, *The Cornell Writer*, where his first published story appeared. He also developed a close friendship with Richard Fariña, who later wrote *Been Down So Long It Looks Like Up to Me*, to whom *Gravity's Rainbow* is dedicated. Several of his early stories, including "The Small Rain," "Mortality and Mercy in Vienna," "Under the Rose," and "Entropy," were written during this period.

After graduation Pynchon turned down offers of a Woodrow Wilson Fellowship, a position teaching creative writing at Cornell, and a job as a film critic with *Esquire* to live a bohemian existence in Greenwich Village while working on his first novel, *V.* He took a job as an engineering aide with the Boeing Co. in Seattle from 1960 to 1962, then lived in California and Mexico while he finished *V.*, which was published in 1963 and won the William Faulkner Foundation Award.

The Crying of Lot 49 followed in 1966 and won the Rosenthal Foundation Award of the National Institute of Arts and Letters. Pynchon's masterpiece and last work of fiction to date, *Gravity's Rainbow*, was published in 1973. Together with a collection of stories by Isaac Bashevis Singer it was co-winner of the National Book Award. Preserving his privacy, Pynchon sent "Professor" Irwin Corey, a master of comic double-talk, to accept the prize, to the consternation of the audience. Although the judges of the Pulitzer Prize were unanimous in selecting *Gravity's Rainbow*, the Pulitzer Advisory Board overruled them. They branded the novel as "unreadable," "turgid," "over-written," and "obscene" and gave no prize that year. In 1975 *Gravity's Rainbow* was awarded the Howells Medal of the National Institute of Arts and Letters and the American Academy of Arts and Letters. Pynchon declined it, stating, "The Howells Medal is a great honor, and, being gold, probably a good hedge against inflation, too. But I don't want it. Please don't impose on me something I don't want. It makes the Academy look arbitrary and me look rude. . . . I know I should behave with more class, but there appears to be only one way to say no, and that's no."

James Joyce's dictum that the artist should be re-fined out of existence seems to have been taken liter-ally by Pynchon: only one photograph of him exists; his dossier at Cornell has mysteriously vanished; and records of his service in the navy were burned in a fire at the records office in St. Louis. He eludes scholarly detectives and sycophantic worshipers by going under assumed names and continuously changing addresses. His reclusiveness has spawned a rumor mill regarding who and where he is and what his next work will be about. Regarding his next novel, a rampant rumor holds that it will concern the *Mothra* movies, a series of Japanese monster films about a benevolent giant moth and its two miniature female attendants. Pyn-chon, of course, remains silent. Over a dozen years

THE AUTHOR AS LUDDITE

have now passed since the publication of *Gravity's Rainbow*, but, whether or not any new masterwork appears from Pynchon's pen, he has already earned a significant place in American letters.

Overview

Pynchon's works are concerned in large part with the act of naming as an attempt to identify or to attain identity and with the limitations that are inherent in the completion of that act. This concern coincides with the post–World War II literary redefinition of realism and places Pynchon at the forefront of contemporary fiction writers. Naming attempts to order the flux of life, to make sense of a shifting array of signs to derive meaning. In a world that ironically is rendered more confusing by its exponential increase of available information, this attempt is heroic. Yet the imposition of a name involves a selection that encapsulates a process, thereby presenting the equivalent of a snapshot view of experience. While the act itself is creative—the coining of metaphors as aids to interpretation—its results are often sterile. The rational impulse to substantiate such selections becomes an effort to systematize that is often exclusive. A system will frequently metamorphose from a cultural methodology to a way of thinking, a metaphysic, thereby dictating hierarchies of abstract concepts by which to judge individual value.

Pynchon creates his characters as extremes, often pairing approaches to living that are antithetical without permitting any synthesis of views. One dominant metaphor is the hothouse/street duality in which characters either choose to seal themselves within a protective and unchanging environment or to participate in the chaotic mutability that defines the outside world. Either extreme is inherently self-deluding in its attempt to impose meaning and comments on the process of fiction writing as an act of naming. Pynchon's fictions remind his readers of the limitation of rationalism because they resist fixed interpretations. At the conclusion of *The Crying of Log 49*, Oedipa Maas ponders several possible causes for her predicament, and we end the novel with her still awaiting revelation. In *V.* the investigation of the various historical incarnations of Thanatos invites theories of a conspiracy of darkness while demonstrating how such paranoia, while apparently justified, abets entropic decay. Following the lead of Henry Adams, Pynchon adapts the term *entropy* (from Newton's second law of thermodynamics that all things tend toward maximum disorder or entropy) to a cultural context that is also reflected in his style. *Gravity's Rainbow* generally refuses to indulge its readers with the comfort of transitions and presents a protean protagonist who even-

THE AUTHOR AS LUDDITE

tually disappears from the novel. At one point in *Gravity's Rainbow*, Pynchon suddenly breaks the spell of his novel to chastise his readers for their reliance on cause and effect. Our struggles to come to terms with what his works mean also become self-referential and comment on the travesty of rigid intellectual constructs.

Increasingly Pynchon's novels focus on the ramifications of Calvinism, particularly as a rational system that has been transmuted to the death force of colonialism. By assigning value according to polarities of the elect and the damned, Calvinism engages in abstract distinctions that negate the vitality of the fluctuating middle ground that it excludes. Many of Pynchon's characters traverse this middle ground and are often victimized by the controlling system that strives to assign them a fixed identity. Those who succumb are rendered essentially inanimate, and some take perverse pleasure in adapting their bodies to match their mechanical mentalities. Any possible escape is associated with humanistic responses to life's entrapments. In *V.*, McClintic Sphere advises Paola Maijstral to "keep cool, but care." Oedipa Maas contemplates shifting dynamics through a metaphor from differential calculus while helping a drunk to complete an act of communication. And the protean Tyrone Slothrop of *Gravity's Rainbow* attains the status of mythological and comic book hero in combatting oppression. These characters are revitalized after undergoing a descent into the underworld of their culture. There they draw sustenance from the rich vein of metaphors that the system-mongers have labeled waste because it threatens the fixed poles of belief upon which they premise their control.

Pynchon's fascination with underground movements throughout history informs the substance and style of his fiction. He attacks the empirical determinacy that dominates the western world view through his satire of characters that rely on it and through his own violations of narrative convention. In doing so, Pynchon depicts the dangers of overreliance on rationalism and sympathizes with the practitioners of a type of anarchic humanism. By shattering the security of simplistic and sterile dualities, he removes us from our reliance on predetermined names and demands that we engage in the creative act of naming.

In a recent essay entitled "Is It O.K. to Be a Luddite?"—one of few indications since *Gravity's Rainbow* that his pen is alive and well—Pynchon typically relates a historical incident to elucidate a cultural cusp. The Luddites, he tells us, were bands of men who flourished in Britain between 1811 and 1816 and whose object was to destroy the machinery that was replacing them in the textile industry. They detached themselves from the British ruler and swore allegiance only to their mythical King Ludd. Ludd derived his

THE AUTHOR AS LUDDITE

name from one Ned Lud, who "in 1779, in a village somewhere in Leicestershire . . . broke into a house and 'in a fit of insane rage' destroyed two machines used for knitting hosiery." Pynchon goes on to relate this group of counterrevolutionaries to a persistent but repressed mode of thought in western culture that refers back to the Age of Miracles in seeking a Hermetic unity and that denies the divisiveness inherent in the rational arrangement of a mechanical universe.

Pynchon's works are full of Luddites and are themselves written in Luddite spirit. His novels undercut the intellectual parochialism that regulates the cultural machinery. In them the act of storytelling becomes the act of naming, a means for miracle. But, like most parables and miracles, they are paradoxical. Pynchon's reminders that we are participating in a fictional construct constitute entrapments that deny closure. His anti-empirical posture recognizes the necessity of lies to discover truth.

As underground characters Pynchon's protagonists are Luddites on a quest with little direction. They seek escape and attain discovery, usually by accident. Joining the repressed, they become fictional freedom fighters who attack restrictive rational conventions. Pynchon also presents those who quest after control, largely as an outgrowth of their obsession with self-control. Through his portrayal of these authorities, the self-appointed and self-perpetuating elect, Pynchon reflects cultural perversions. His assessment is not, however, a simple polarity, for both groups are adorned with cultural paraphernalia that is largely dictated by those in control, whose pernicious influence becomes an omnipresent conspiracy, a burgeoning infection elicited through inevitable contact.

Pynchon's works are Luddite plots to convert his readers. They disrupt our reliance on rational norms by graphically depicting some of the gruesome by-products of those norms. We witness the enslavement of reason as a tool for self-aggrandizement and the consequent permutations of destruction. Pynchon locates colonial repression as a compensatory reaction to the fear and self-hatred of the colonists, and portrays a self-perpetuating death wish giving rise to or having arisen from (he suggests both possibilities) some cosmic malevolence. Colonialism becomes more than a practice of governments; it is revealed as a metaphysic within the western psyche. Pynchon confronts us with our own preconceptions and shows us their manifestations. His self-referentiality forces an equivalent reader response by exposing our indulgence in lies.

Through his myriad authorial poses Pynchon preserves a certain anonymity in literature and in life. In addition to black humorist, fabulist, encyclopedist, detective, and mercurial delinquent, he is a moralist. Just as many of his characters rummage in literal and

THE AUTHOR AS LUDDITE

figurative rubbish, he finds value in the denigrated aspects of our cultural history. Fascinated with underground challenges to authority and inversions of order, he also scrutinizes minutiae in search of the sacred. Pynchon, however, presents his revelations piecemeal, permitting us no certitude in discovery. A self-effacing prophet of doom, he is the recording conscience of our demise as a culture and the voice of salvational alternatives. One critic has called him "the greatest living writer in the English-speaking world."[2] The power of Pynchon's message and the revolutionary impact of his method of presentation justify this accolade.

Notes

1. Mathew Winston, "The Quest for Pynchon," *Twentieth Century Literature* 21, 3 (1975): 280.

2. Edward Mendelson, introduction, *Pynchon: A Collection of Critical Essays*, ed. Edward Mendelson (Englewood Cliffs, NJ: Prentice-Hall, 1978) 15.

CHAPTER TWO

Slow Learner: Establishing Foundations

Slow Learner collects five of Pynchon's early stories, outlining his writer's apprenticeship. Taken with his entertaining and candid introduction to the collection, they offer an excellent guideline for the aspiring writer, much like a postmodern version of Rilke's *Letters to a Young Poet.* Even though Pynchon wrote "The Secret Integration" after the publication of *V.,* all the stories possess the flaws of undergraduate pieces. "My specific piece of wrong procedure back then," he admits, "was, incredibly, to browse through the thesaurus and note words that sounded cool, hip, or likely to produce an effect, usually that of making me look good, without then taking the trouble to go and find out in the dictionary what they meant."[1] Pynchon's showmanship, especially his insistence on calling attention to literary allusions, is unrestrained. Unlike most undergraduate works, however, these stories are brilliantly conceived, although unevenly executed. As is typical of a thoughtful and probing

SLOW LEARNER

young man, he forces concepts on structures that will not hold them. Yet the reader is fortunate to be able to witness his process of discovery. In these stories one can observe his sometimes fumbling but consistently penetrating attempts to tunnel into the subterranean underpinnings of our culture. He frequently presents his disturbing findings like a stand-up comic, sometimes betraying his lack of confidence by playing too strongly to his audience. But in his comedy there is always conscience, born of seriousness and fear and wonder.

In Pynchon's first published story, "The Small Rain" (1959), the "characters are found dealing with death in pre-adult ways" (5). Like numerous characters in his novels these retreat from feeling: "they evade: they sleep late, they seek euphemisms. When they do mention death they try to make with the jokes. Worst of all, they hook it up with sex." Nathan "Lardass" Levine acquires autobiographical dimensions, having "once dug Lester Young or Gerry Mulligan at Birdland" and being "over six feet and loose jointed" (28). A graduate of the City College of New York, he has enlisted in the army and is stationed at Fort Roach, Louisiana. Levine enjoys the inertia of army life in the middle of nowhere. He passes his time reading pornographic novels like *Swamp Wench* while specializing in mental inanition. Ironically, he is a communications expert, thereby introducing Pynchon's fascination with the relationship between communication and entropy.

Levine is jerked from his self-enclosure when a hurricane strikes southern Louisiana and his unit is ordered into action. Confronted with the decaying corpses that must be dragged from the water, he plunges from a psychological wasteland into a literal one: "one [corpse] they unhooked from a barbed wire fence. It hung there like a foolish balloon, a travesty; until they touched it and it popped, hissed and collapsed" (47). Furthermore, the students at the college campus where the army takes up residence during the disaster are oblivious to the horror that surrounds them, thereby commenting on Levine's own death-in-life. Lest the reader miss the point, Pynchon self-consciously alludes to T. S. Eliot and Ernest Hemingway to expand this localized situation to universal proportions.

Levine's immersion in this atmosphere of death transforms him. No longer able to derive comfort from evasion, he envisions himself as "Lardass Levine the Wandering Jew, debating on weekday evenings in strange and nameless towns with other Wandering Jews the essential problems of identity" (49). The influence of Jack Kerouac's *On the Road* is certainly here, and Pynchon also points to Helen Waddell's *The Wandering Scholars*, which discusses a group of medieval poets who departed from their cloistered monasteries to experience the broader dimensions of life in the outside world (7–8). Levine's vision projects the outlines of Benny Profane, Tyrone Slothrop, and all the perpetual malcontents that stream through Pynchon's fiction, seeking identity in a world that negates it.

Toward the end of the story Levine drives off with a teasing coed who calls herself Little Buttercup. They drive to a cabin in the swamp where she becomes the incarnation of his swamp wench, "a never totally violated Pasiphae" (50) whose lack of touching after the sex act secures her place in the death-in-life labyrinth of avoidance that substitutes for communication. "In the midst of the great death, the little death" (50), Levine says in reference to the seventeenth-century belief that each orgasm diminished one's life by a day. Yet his experience during the disaster also diminishes his interest in returning to Fort Roach at the conclusion of the story. Although he is no Fisher King, we witness in him a temporary rebirth through self-recognition.

While Pynchon self-deprecatingly refers to the narrative voice in "Low-lands" (1960) as that of a "smart-assed jerk who didn't know any better" (12), the story is well structured and rich in suggestion. It extends Pynchon's use of Eliot's "The Waste Land," descending into a fantastic underworld to escape from the surface world's stifling rationality. Tony Tanner calls "Low-lands" a rewriting of Washington Irving's

"Rip Van Winkle."[2] Ironically, however, Pynchon's protagonist enters the dream state through an awakening.

Dennis Flange, a former naval communications officer who is currently a lawyer, stays home from his office to drink muscatel and listen to Vivaldi with the local garbageman, Rocco Squarcione. Much to his wife Cindy's dismay, his former naval buddy, Pig Bodine, appears on the doorstep. Pig becomes Pynchon's archetypal anarchistic slob, and he brings him back for encores in *V.* and *Gravity's Rainbow.* Having lured Flange away on his wedding night seven years ago for a two-week drunken debauch, Pig has been banished by Cindy, who now throws the three men out of the house and tells Flange not to return.

Flange's home life foreshadows the stultifying domesticity that we find on the opening page of *The Crying of Lot 49.* His two-story home is perched on a cliff overlooking the sea; Flange calls it his "womb with a view" (57). It contains concealed passageways and a network of tunnels in the cellar constructed for whiskey-running during Prohibition. However, prohibition in an emotional sense has ascended upstairs, for Flange practices "Molemanship," regressing into fetal positions and inertia. His marriage has attained nothing but bourgeois sterility. Cindy has convinced Flange to purchase a $1,000 stereo system that she uses only as a surface for hors d'oeuvre dishes and cocktail trays.

SLOW LEARNER

Her one-dimensional logic also extends to a fondness for the sharp angles of Mondrian paintings, which she hangs inside a domesticated police booth around which she grows ivy and to which Flange is banished whenever they have a fight.

Flange indulges in two forms of escape from the constraints of his home life. His sessions with his analyst, Geronimo Diaz, depart completely from the over-reliance on rationality that defines his life with Cindy. Diaz is the prototype for Dr. Hilarius of *The Crying of Lot 49* and for the scientists of The White Visitation in *Gravity's Rainbow*. He believes he is Paganini and has lost his powers because he sold his soul to the devil. His sessions with Flange consist of imbibing martinis and "reading aloud to himself out of random-number tables or the Ebbinghaus nonsense-syllable lists, ignoring everything that Flange would be trying to tell him" (58).

Flange's other indulgence is his thoughts of the sea with which he withdraws from the monotony of his life, seeking a cushion for his emotional pain. However, his perspective on the sea lacks the important spatial dimension that he acquires when he descends from his house to arrive at sea level in the dump.

Rocco takes Flange and Pig to the dump, which is presided over by a watchman named Bolingbroke (*Henry IV*) who wears a porkpie hat for a crown. In Bolingbroke's shack they swap sea stories over wine in a scene reminiscent of the "Eumaeus" episode of *Ulysses*.[3] Ironically, the story that Flange tells bears no relation to the sea, but recounts a fraternity prank with a stolen female cadaver. His reason for relating this type of story asserts his passivity as a metaphysic:

But the real reason he knew and could not say was that if you are Dennis Flange and if the sea's tides are the same that not only wash along your veins but also billow through your fantasies then it is all right to listen to but not to tell stories about that sea, because you and the truth of a true lie were thrown sometime way back into a curious contiguity and as long as you are passive you can remain aware of the truth's extent but the minute you become active you are somehow, if not violating a convention outright, at least screwing up the perspective of things, much as anyone observing subatomic particles changes the works, data and odds, by the act of observing. So he had told the other instead, at random. Or apparently so (69).

Flange invokes Werner Heisenberg's uncertainty principle, which holds that the position of a subatomic particle cannot be precisely determined without disrupting the system, for the paired qualities of position and motion cannot be measured concurrently. For Flange, life and fantasy are precariously balanced, a balance preserved by passivity. To tell a sea story would be to bring the fantasy world to an active level and thus to disrupt the equilibrium of the duality.

SLOW LEARNER

The dump is situated fifty feet below street level, a "low-lands," which Flange associates with a Scottish sea chanty:

> A ship I have got in the North Country
> And she goes by the name of the *Golden Vanity*,
> O, I fear she will be taken by a Spanish Gal-la-lee,
> As she sails by the Low-lands low.

In descending from the perspective of his house above the sea to that of the dump at sea level, Flange attains an epiphany through his observation of the borderless expanse of debris:

Any arrival at sea level was like finding a minimum and dimensionless point, a unique crossing of parallel and meridian, an assurance of perfect, passionless uniformity; just as in the spiraling descent of Rocco's truck he had felt that this spot at which they finally came to rest was the dead center, the single point which implied an entire low country. Whenever he was away from Cindy and could think he would picture his life as a surface in the process of change, much as the floor of the dump was in transition: from concavity or inclosure to perhaps a flatness like the one he stood in now. What he worried about was any eventual convexity, a shrinking, it might be, of the planet itself to some palpable curvature of whatever he would be standing on, so that he would be left sticking out like a projected radius, unsheltered and reeling across the empty lunes of his tiny sphere (65–66).

The flat perspective allows him to project his imagination without limitation. The civilizing process, however, is equated to the piling of debris on the dump site, a process that alters the flat perspective and creates the "convexity" that is at the root of Flange's fear. Like the Mondrian angles that preside over the solitude of his sleep, civilized rationality imposes immediate horizons on the free and open perspectives of his fantasy life.

Flange's recognition permits him acccess to his alter ego, or doppelgänger, as he awakens to a siren voice calling, "Anglo, . . . Anglo with the golden hair. Come out. Come out by the secret path and find me" (72). He leaves the shack, but knocks over a stack of snow tires arranged by Bolingbroke as a booby trap for gypsies. His revival from unconsciousness is accomplished by a beautiful, three-and-a-half-foot "angel" named Nerissa, suggesting both Portia's maid in *The Merchant of Venice* and a mythical sea nymph. She then leads him through a network of underground tunnels emanating from a backless GE refrigerator to her home. The underground complex, he learns, was built in the thirties by a revolutionary group called the Sons of the Red Apocalypse and has been occupied by gypsies since their demise. In her abode Flange encounters her pet rat, Hyacinth, a forerunner of the rat Veronica in *V.* Nerissa reveals that a fortune-teller named Violetta had foretold that Flange would be her

SLOW LEARNER

husband, and the story concludes with Flange deciding to stay. He looks at Nerissa and sees sea images: "whitecaps danced across her eyes; sea creatures, he knew, would be cruising about in the submarine green of her heart" (77). His transformation into his fantasy world is complete.

The references to Eliot's poem are numerous. Joseph Slade argues that Flange is the Phoenician sailor who travels in the wasteland. Violetta is Madame Sosostris, and Nerissa the hyacinth girl who offers renewal.[4] The conclusion of the story also suggests the vision of the mermaids at the end of "The Love Song of J. Alfred Prufrock." However, Prufrock's dream life fails to redeem him, while Flange's fantasy offers a positive alternative to the mundane void of his life with Cindy. His vision of Nerissa and the rat as children counterpoints the sterility of his marriage, with the resultant conviction that "a child makes it all right. Let the world shrink to a *boccie* ball" (76). This image, drawn from Marvell's "To His Coy Mistress," indicates a commitment to life rather than a retreat. In this sense Slade's argument that the story is static is fallacious.[5] Instead, Thomas Schaub's contention that it possesses an hourglass shape, so that the ending becomes an inverted mirror of the beginning, appears more accurate.[6] Flange's descent into the underworld of his fantasy life is a return to the imagination's primal wellspring, unencumbered by the sharp angles of rationality that had previously punctured his security.

In his introduction to *Slow Learner*, Pynchon points to the primary weakness in "Entropy" (1960): "It is simply wrong to begin with a theme, symbol or other abstract unifying agent, and then to try to force characters and events to conform to it" (12). The abstract unifying agent is stated in the title, and its cultural and metaphysical applications, derived from Pynchon's reading of *The Education of Henry Adams* and Norbert Wiener's *The Human Use of Human Beings*, are suggested by the depressing climate depicted in the epigraph from Henry Miller's *Tropic of Cancer*. References to literature that depicts sexual perversion—de Sade, Faulkner's *Sanctuary*, Djuna Barnes's *Nightwood*—further underscore the theme of decay. While the characters, as Pynchon admits, "come off as synthetic, insufficiently alive" (13), the story is nonetheless important because it is the first full treatment of thematic material that is to form the cornerstone of Pynchon's novels.

Given the combination of engineering and literature in Pynchon's education, the significance of Eliot's "The Waste Land" to his writing is logically succeeded by that of Henry Adams's theories. Adams applies the second law of thermodynamics—that all things tend toward disorder or entropy—to the decay of civilization. Entropy manifests itself in two somewhat para-

SLOW LEARNER

doxical ways. In one sense order breaks down, resulting in the random dispersement of energy. In the other the distinctions between the elements of a closed system vanish, resulting in a sterile homogeneity. Adams's applications of these physical laws to his observations of culture form definitive metaphors with which Pynchon structures his future work.

The frequent musical references in the story comment upon its fuguelike structure: the events on two floors of a Washington, D.C. apartment building are counterpointed. On the lower floor Meatball Mulligan is giving a raucous lease-breaking party that has entered its second day. Entropic chaos builds as new guests, primarily government workers, coeds, and sailors, arrive. One woman falls asleep in the sink, and, when moved to the shower, she sits on the drain and almost drowns from the rising water. However, this chaos does not occur within a closed system since diversity is constantly added to the apartment party from the street outside. Given two alternatives to dealing with the mess that his party has become— locking himself in the closet until everyone goes away or trying to calm his guests by attending to their individual needs—Meatball chooses the latter. In choosing not to seal himself off from participation in the flux of life and the diversity of the street, he foreshadows the advice that Oedipa Maas receives in *The Crying of Lot 49* to "keep it bouncing," thereby avoiding deterioration into the lifeless sameness that constitutes the entropic system.

In contrast, the apartment on the floor above houses Callisto and Aubade, who live in a "hothouse" environment. Isolating himself from the world, Callisto creates a closed and unchanging system—an entropic state:

Hermetically sealed, it was a tiny enclave of regularity in the city's chaos, alien to the vagaries of the weather, of national politics, of any civil disorder. Through trial-and-error Callisto had perfected its ecological balance, with the help of the girl its artistic harmony, so that the swayings of its plant life, the stirrings of its birds and human inhabitants were all as integral as the rhythms of a perfectly-executed mobile. He and the girl could no longer, of course, be omitted from that sanctuary; they had become necessary to its unity. What they needed from outside was delivered. They did not go out (83–84).

Because the temperature outside has registered 37 degrees for three days, Callisto conjures a paranoiac vision of the heat death of the universe. His obsession fills his memoirs, which he dictates to Aubade, Henry Adams style, in the third person.[7] However, Aubade hears noises from the street and the music from the party punctuating Callisto's words: "the architectonic purity of her world was constantly threatened by such

hints of anarchy" (88). She is part French and part An-
namese and therefore contains the capacity to bring
together two worlds. This, plus the musical aspect of
her name, casts her in the symbolic role of harmoni-
zer. As the story alternates between Mulligan's party
and Callisto's apartment, the reader learns that Callisto is attempting to heal a sick bird by holding it
against the heat of his body, thereby resisting mutability. The eventual death of the bird signals the destruction of the self-contained ecological balance in the
room, and Aubade smashes the window to allow the
outside world to penetrate.

While Meatball restores order to his party by caring for his guests, Callisto's act of love toward the bird
fails to prevent disorder. Seeking an equilibrium between inside and out, Aubade permits the street to invade the hothouse uninhibited. Like the protagonists
of all of Pynchon's novels, Meatball and Aubade com-
bat personal and cultural entropy by choosing between hothouse and street. They also share with these
later characters the fact that their triumphs are often
Pyrrhic and always ephemeral.

"Under the Rose" (1961), later reworked as chapter 3 of *V.*, offers an early indication of Pynchon's capacity to piece together historical events within a
fictional narrative. The novel's version includes significant alterations. Most importantly, the events are
narrated through the perspective of Herbert Stencil,

whose obsessive quest for V. causes him to focus on Victoria Wren so that the other characters serve primarily as a backdrop. The novel does not depict, for example, Porpentine's discovery that Goodfellow's Lothario image is a sham when he observes his impotent tryst with Victoria. Nor does it explore Porpentine's compassion, which is also his fatal flaw.

"Under the Rose" is set in Cairo at the time of the Fashoda crisis in 1898, when the British and French were vying for the strategic area in the Upper Nile. The British spies, Porpentine and Goodfellow, attempt to ward off any terrorist acts that might ignite war. Germany, on the other hand, has much to gain from a war between Britain and France. It sends a trio of spies—Lepsius, Bongo-Shaftsbury, and Mold-weorp[8]—to assassinate the English consul-general, Lord Cromer, in an attempt to encourage hostilities.

The British spies have been trained in a tradition where espionage is conducted on a "gentlemanly basis" (102). Despite their opposed allegiances both British and German agents share a code of conduct. They are "comrade Machiavellians, still playing the games of Renaissance Italian politics in a world that has outgrown them" (107). This code centers around an absolutely impersonal approach to the work of espionage and a consequent disdain for the impurities of human feelings. Bongo-Shaftsbury physically converts to a mechanical doll to cleanse himself of his humanity.

Similarly, Moldweorp responds to a prostitute's proposition with a vicious assault. Like Bongo-Shaftsbury he favors "the clean over the impure" (117). Pynchon develops here a theme that will dominate his novels: the transformation in world view from the dominance of the human to that of the inanimate, a reworking of Henry Adams's metaphors of Virgin and Dynamo. The reader observes this shift in microcosm when Porpentine meditates on the new generation of spies:

Time was his fellow professionals became adept through practice. Learned ciphers by breaking them, custom officials by evading them, some opponents by killing them. Now the new ones read books: young lads, full of theory and (he'd decided) a faith in nothing but the perfection of their own internal machinery (123).

Porpentine dies because he breaks the code of espionage by permitting his feelings to interfere with his work. He and Goodfellow attempt to frustrate the Germans' assassination of Lord Cromer while Cromer attends a performance of Puccini's *Manon Lescaut* at the Cairo opera house. Pynchon's habit of milking his allusions for all they are worth is illustrated by his choice of this particular opera, which comments on the characters and events of the story. The hero, Des

Grieux, who had previously rejected the idea of love, is smitten by a beautiful woman and is subsequently victimized by his newfound romanticism. Likewise Porpentine succumbs to human emotions. He responds to Victoria Wren's plea to protect Goodfellow and also expresses personal anger toward a fellow spy.[9] As he leaves the opera house, he violates the code by yelling at Moldweorp to "go away and die" (134). For this he is executed after chasing the Germans across the desert, the setting where Des Grieux also plays his final scene. Before Porpentine is killed, he requests, and is granted, the release of Victoria and Goodfellow. However, the gentlemanly basis for espionage can no longer apply to him: "He'd crossed some threshold without knowing. Mongrel now, no longer pure. . . . Mongrel, he supposed, is only another way of saying human. After the final step you could not, nothing could be, clean" (137).

The story concludes sixteen years later with Goodfellow in Sarajevo, attempting to prevent the assassination of the Archduke Ferdinand, an event that will spark World War I. His age and impotence comment on his ineffectiveness. With the end of the nineteenth century comes the collapse of traditional codes of conduct. The dedicated agent as savior is rendered anachronistic. While Goodfellow clings to the antiquated image of the spy, his latest "conquest" describes him to her friends as "a simple-minded Englishman,

not much good in bed but liberal with his money"
(137). The modern world is of a different order, and
the old rules lack relevance.

"The Secret Integration" (1964) is an initiation
tale set in Mingeborough, Massachusetts, in the Berk-
shire mountains where Pynchon was raised. It involves a group of children who conspire against the
hypocritical institutions that their parents engender.
Grover Snodd, a boy genius in the Salinger mode,
provides the brains behind their plans. He seeks a perfect symmetry of action against the confused patterns
offered by the adults. The inner junta of his group
consists of Tim Santora, from whose point of view the
events are narrated; a practical joker named Étienne
Cherdlu (a variant of Etoain Shrdlu from the linotype
keyboard); a nine-year-old reformed alcoholic named
Hogan Slothrop (Tyrone's brother); and a sixth grader
named Kim Dufay, who is aroused by explosives and
whose size 28A padded bra permits her to pass for an
adult at PTA meetings. Financed by milk money from
other malcontented children who enlist in their cause,
they conduct Operation Spartacus (the title of which
Grover takes from the Stanley Kubrick film). They
drop sodium bombs in school toilets and stir up silt in
the river to stall machines in the local paper mill.
However, many of their acts of sabotage fail because
fear of adult authority is so ingrained in the children.
In one attack on the school several children are halted

by the chalk lines on the playing field which, Grover deduces, remind them of classroom authority.

While Operation Spartacus falters, the story enters a second dimension as Hogan is sent as a joke by the local AA to respond to a call from a black alcoholic, Mr. McAfee. Tim accompanies him, and Grover and Étienne join them later. Hogan's serious response to his assignment moves McAfee, and he exchanges tales with the children. Although he enjoys the spirit of their pranks, his own stories are filled with the isolation caused by his color. His loneliness so affects Tim that he telephones long distance to a girl whose name McAfee has carried in his wallet for years. But, his call for help yields no results, and Tim's innocence is rudely dented:

It was right around then that Tim's foot felt the edge of a certain abyss which he had been walking close to— for who knew how long?—without knowing. He looked over it, got afraid, and shied away, but not before learning something unpleasant about the night: that it was night here, and in New York, and probably on whatever coast the man was talking about, one single night over the entire land, making people, already so tiny in it, invisible too in the dark; and how hard would it be, how hopeless, to really find a person you needed suddenly, unless you lived all your life in a house like he did, with a mother and father (183).

SLOW LEARNER

The police then arrive and unceremoniously run McAfee out of town.

Revenge is in order and the children regroup. Their retaliation is an ingenious imposition of color on the bland security of a random group of adults. They don green masks and place green floodlights along a railroad track, suddenly horrifying a trainload of passengers.

One member of the group is a black boy, Carl Barrington, who is later revealed to be a fantasy figure born out of their collective rejection of adult bigotry. A childless couple, the Barringtons, have recently integrated the neighborhood and are subjected to abusive calls from the parents. When the children attempt to help them clean up a load of garbage that has been dumped in their front yard, they discover objects from their own households.

The only integration that can occur in this repressive environment is secretive. With the perverse views of Mingeborough society fully exposed, Carl is no longer safe, even as a fantasy figure, in the children's homes and school. He goes to live in their hideout, the mansion of King Yrjö, which is inhabited by the seven-foot ghost of the king's aide. Only in this detached refuge can he remain intact. Meanwhile, the other children return to their individual homes, to a "hot shower, dry towel, before-bed television, good

night kiss, and dreams that could never again be entirely safe" (193).

Notes

1. Thomas Pynchon, *Slow Learner* (Boston: Little, Brown, 1984) 15.
Further references will be noted parenthetically.

2. Tony Tanner, *Thomas Pynchon* (New York: Methuen, 1982) 31.

3. David Seed makes this astute connection in "Fantasy and Dream in
Thomas Pynchon's 'Low-lands,' " *Rocky Mountain Review* 37, 1–2 (1983):
61. John O. Stark discusses the self-reflexive nature of the stories within
the story in *Pynchon's Fictions* (Athens: Ohio University Press, 1980):
161–65.

4. Joseph W. Slade, *Thomas Pynchon* (New York: Warner, 1974) 28–
31.

5. Slade 25.

6. Thomas H. Schaub, "Where Have We Been, Where Are We Headed?
A Retrospective View of Pynchon Criticism," *Pynchon Notes* 7 (Oct.
1983): 12–13.

7. David Seed discusses parallels between the relationship of Callisto
and Aubade and that of Hamm and Clov in Beckett's *Endgame* ("Order in
Thomas Pynchon's 'Entropy,' " *Journal of Narrative Technique* 11 ([1981]:
138–39).

8. Pynchon writes in his introduction to *Slow Learner:* "Attentive
fans of Shakespeare will notice that the name Porpentine is lifted from
Hamlet, I, v. It is an early form of 'porcupine.' The name Moldweorp is
Old Teutonic for 'mole'—the animal, not the infiltrator. I thought it would
be a cute idea for people named after two amiable fuzzy critters to be duk-
ing it out over the fate of Europe" (19).

9. David Cowart offers a full discussion of the significance of *Manon
Lescaut* to "Under the Rose" in *Thomas Pynchon: The Art of Allusion*
(Carbondale: Southern Illinois University Press, 1980) 65–72

CHAPTER THREE

"An Eye That Reflects and an Eye That Receives": Vision and Anti-Vision in *V.*

Pynchon's first novel, *V.*, is a coincidence of contraries with no reconciliation, a mockery of the act of reading, a hub without a wheel. Narrative legerdemain fragments both plot and reader and simultaneously recapitulates and undercuts theme. Pynchon wrote the novel while employed as a technical writer at Boeing (which he embraces in his mythography as Yoyodyne) in Seattle, his dual background in literature and engineering contributing to an interest in Norbert Wiener's study of the relationship between man and machine—cybernetics. In *V.*, Pynchon blends metaphors derived from Wiener's *The Human Use of Human Beings*, Henry Adams's *Education*, and Robert Graves's *The White Goddess*, along with smatterings of Ludwig Wittgenstein, T. S. Eliot, Vladimir

Nabokov, and Nathanael West to create a context that ironically questions the purpose of metaphor. The humor permeating *V.*'s grim world view is reminiscent of the advice of Twain's mysterious stranger that "against the assault of laughter nothing can stand." However, *V.* inverts the formula. In Twain, as in Henri Bergson's essay "Laughter," comedy dismisses the encroachment of the inanimate on the human.[1] But in Pynchon black humor rings as the animate succumbs to the mechanical, making comedy an adjunct to nihilism and eliminating it as a means of salvation. Yet the apocalyptic tag most critics have attached to *V.* is too one-dimensional to fit Pynchon's vision. To use Pynchon's term, this tag "stencilizes" *V.* much as the novel imposes on Herbert Stencil's quest a flawed methodology, one that ultimately dupes the quester or necessitates that he dupe himself. Although Pynchon frames Stencil's story in malevolent conspiracy and Benny Profane's in ineluctable accident, advancing both with horrific connotations, he also injects hope for the human through the characters he presents as alternatives to the death force of *V.*[2]

In the epilogue of the novel, narrated through Herbert Stencil's questionable point of view, his father, Sidney, ruminates that "sometime between 1859 and 1919, the world contracted a disease which no one ever took the trouble to diagnose because the symptoms were too subtle—blending in with the events of

VISION AND ANTI-VISION IN *V.*

history, no different one by one but altogether—fatal."[3] This disease, a death force that catalyzes the metastasis of the inanimate and constitutes the fascist *Zeitgeist*,[4] is personified in the metamorphoses of V. V. is an archetypal Terrible Mother who fulfills the entropic prophecies of Henry Adams for the twentieth century. According to Adams, the period of positive human endeavor initially inspired by the cult of the Virgin in the twelfth century was inverting into a modern death wish motivated by the Dynamo. As the supremacy of science replaces that of religion, multiplicity usurps unity. V. unites both the Dynamo and the Virgin, rendering the creative powers of the divine Feminine destructive. V.'s incarnations occur at various trouble spots in modern history. Whether the Fashoda crisis of 1898 in Cairo, the riots at the Venezuelan embassy in Florence in 1899, Paris on the eve of World War I in 1913, German-occupied Southwest Africa in 1922, or Malta during the Second World War and the Suez crisis, V.'s natural habitat is "the state of siege" (62). Herbert Stencil's obsession with her, a quest for a toxic Grail, begins as an apparent accident while leafing through his father's journals in 1945. After spending forty-four years as an "itinerant somnambulist," Stencil converts the drift of his life into an all-encompassing career. His tracking of V. may also be read as a simultaneous search for and escape from his own identity as well as that of modern man.

Like Henry Adams, Stencil refers to himself in the third person, an objectification that suggests his distance from a secure sense of identity. Pynchon implants the suggestion that Stencil's search for V. is also a search for his mother. In her incarnation as Victoria Wren in Florence in 1899, V. seduced Sidney Stencil. While the possibility that Herbert is the product of this tryst requires a pregnancy of well over a year, since he was born in 1901, V.'s powers transcend human limitations.

Although Stencil discovers his career by accident, his obsession generates a paranoid theory that seemingly random events are actually parts of a malevolent conspiracy over which V. presides. His attempts to translate history into a linear and fixed pattern reflect a "hothouse" mentality, one of the extremes between which the twentieth century is caught. V. is a study in intellectual fetishism, and the hothouse attempt to dwell in memory by reductively viewing experience is one of the most destructive of fetishes. By gathering the myriad forms of experience under a single rubric, hothouse stencilizations impose meaning; they stultify rather than illuminate. Still, Pynchon does not demonstrate them to be false. Hothouse interpretations become a series of fictions, costumes in which to dress segments chosen from the flow of history in order to cloak them with meaning. Yet these constructs of meaning are a necessary part of the human endeavor to make sense of the world.

VISION AND ANTI-VISION IN *V.*

In this respect Norbert Wiener's analogy between humans and communication machines may be relevant to Pynchon's novel: "It is my thesis that the physical functioning of the living individual and the operation of some of the newer communication machines are precisely parallel in their analogous attempts to control entropy through feedback. Both of them have sensory receptors as one stage in their cycle of operation: that is, in both of them there exists a special apparatus for collecting information from the outer world at low energy levels, and for making it available in the operation of the individual or of the machine. . . . The information is then turned into a form available for the further stages of performance. In both of them their *performed* action on the outer world, and not merely their *intended* action, is reported back to the central regulatory apparatus".[5]

In attempting "to control entropy through feedback," Stencil lapses into a hothouse mentality, one where the degree of control limits the flow of information or minimizes the possibilities that that information may generate. To the degree that Stencil's obsessive quest mirrors that of Ahab in *Moby-Dick*, Pynchon is demonstrating Wiener's position that the attempt to control entropy tends to degenerate into an obsession with eradicating evil, a covert Manicheanism.[6] This type of paranoia produces an alienation from the present that causes one to live in a vacuum. Because Stencil's entire conception of life and living is predicated on his search for V., his greatest fear is that his quest will end, that the reality of V. will overtake his illusions. Thus he is reluctant to visit Malta: "His father died in Valletta. He tried to tell himself meeting V. and dying were separate and unconnected for Sidney" (386). When the clues to V. begin to converge, Stencil leaves Malta for Stockholm in pursuit of "one Mme. Viola, oneiromancer and hypnotist" (451). For him the importance of maintaining the mystery has attained dominance over the need to solve it.

Opposed to the historical chapters as interpreted by Stencil are the chapters set in the contemporary America of 1955–56. Modeled on the black humor of Nathanael West, they offer Benny Profane, a schlemihl, as their protagonist. Profane is a wanderer without a destination. Unlike Stencil, who fashions his life in pursuit of a woman, Profane searches for no one: "women had always happened to Profane the schlemihl like accidents: broken shoelaces, dropped dishes, pins in new shirts" (134). While conspiracy rules Stencil's world view, accidents rule Profane's. While Stencil pursues an elusive proselytizer of the inanimate, Profane is consistently plagued by mechanical objects.

The Profane chapters counter the insulation of the hothouse with the open arena of the street. Rather than the zone of memory, the street is a nonselective present. Its mode of motion is termed yo-yoing be-

VISION AND ANTI-VISION IN *V.*

cause of a lack of direction or progress. Like the hot-house the street elicits alienation, and its complete absence of positive or negative spiritual associations, its profane level, ultimately fills it with meaningless-ness. Herbert Stencil reports an entry in his father's journal:

If there is any political moral to be found in this world, . . . it is that we carry on the business of this century with an intolerable double vision. Right and Left; the hothouse and the street. The Right can only live and work hermetically, in the hothouse of the past, while outside the Left prosecute their affairs in the streets by manipulated mob violence. And cannot live but in the dreamscape of the future (468).

While Benny Profane decides that all political events have "the desire to get laid as their roots" (214), Sidney Stencil's more sophisticated vision is no less cynical. Any inflexible extreme when made a world view results in a fixation on a void.

Even the sewer, the realm under the street where fantasy can contribute fresh perspective and imagina-tive intensity, as depicted in Fausto Maijstral's confes-sions, is dangerous when it becomes an absolute, as demonstrated by Father Fairing's parish. Typical of Pynchon's undercutting of narrative authority, Fair-ing's story is told through Profane's point of view when Profane is on Alligator Patrol, hunting the alligators once purchased as babies at pet stores and subsequently flushed down toilets to grow and lumber through the sewers of New York. During the Depression, Fairing decides that the rats were eventually going to control New York, and he begins to live in the sewer in a campaign to convert them to Roman Catholicism. His perspective shattered by the intensity of his commitment, Fairing "considered it small enough sacrifice on their part to provide three of their own per day for physical sustenance, in return for the spiritual nourishment he was giving them" (118). His journal suggests a sexual relationship with one devotee, a female rat named Veronica (after the saint who, when Christ was carrying the cross, wiped his face with a cloth which received an imprint of his countenance), "a kind of voluptuous Magdalen" (121). That Veronica may be one of several perverse incarnations of V. is only suggested by her name and by V.'s ability to appear in situations of destruction and decay. Pynchon maneuvers readers into making this connection while simultaneously reminding them that to indulge too strongly in the suggestion is to fall prey to the paranoid absolutism of a Stencil or a Fairing.

In his two major characters Pynchon personifies the destructive extremes that characterize the twentieth century. Although it has been suggested that Pynchon is invoking the meeting of opposites characterized by Leopold Bloom and Stephen Dedalus in *Ulysses* by having Stencil and Profane travel together to Malta in the last chapter,[7] this coincidence of contraries offers no reconciliation, no symbolic affirmation. Paola Maijstral, a figure of possible salvation, may be linked with Penelope through her promise to her husband, Pappy Hod, to "sit home in Norfolk, faithful, and spin" (443), but *V.* concludes with a destructive waterspout, not a string of yesses.

Like a prophet of doom, crazed by his prophesies into perverse humor, Pynchon portrays the encroachment of the inanimate on twentieth-century life, a conversion of the Garden to the Machine. In a dream Profane recalls a story of a boy with a golden screw in his navel who for twenty years searches for a way to extract it. When the magic screwdriver is found and the curse lifted, the boy jumps out of bed and his ass falls off:

To Profane, alone in the street, it would always seem maybe he was looking for something too to make the fact of his own disassembly plausible as that of any machine. It was always at this point that the fear started: here that it would turn into a nightmare. Because now, if he kept going down that street, not only his ass but also his arms, legs, sponge brain and clock of a heart must be left behind (40).

Two computers, SHROUD (Synthetic Human Radiation Output Determined) and SHOCK (Synthetic

Human Objects Causality Kinematics) of sinister-sounding Anthroresearch Associates, present mirrors of the soulless future of Profane and, by extension, of mankind. At one point Profane hallucinates a conversation with SHROUD in which the computer mockingly reveals the animate nature of humans to be illusory.

As an example of the degeneracy into the inanimate, the Whole Sick Crew offers disaffected "romanticism in its furthest decadence," with its members impersonating "poverty, rebellion, and artistic 'soul,' " while "most of them worked for a living and obtained the substance of their conversation from the pages of Time magazine" (56—57). Fergus Mixolydian wires himself to the TV, his sleep patterns controlling its operation. Slab paints as a Catatonic Expressionist, produces endless portraits of cheese danishes, and refers to his work as "the ultimate in non-communication" (56). Rachel Owlglass makes love to her MG. Indeed, sex becomes mechanical and love displaced onto objects for these characters. At the Sailor's Grave bar sailors celebrate Suck Hour by fighting for access to beer taps shaped like large breasts. Mafia Winsome, a parody of Ayn Rand, writes popular novels of heroic love between "godlike, inexhaustible sex athletes" (126) while plying her own sexual insatiability. Since she is unable to accept her own or others' human flaws, Mafia's love life becomes a series of unfulfilling

VISION AND ANTI-VISION IN *V.*

orgies and her writing the proliferation of unrealizable fantasies.

V. extends prosthetics from a technological advancement to a metaphysic. Pynchon mimics Dryden's depiction in *The Medall* of the Earl of Shaftesbury in his portrayal of the spy, Bongo-Shaftsbury. Dryden satirized Shaftesbury as "Tapski" and played with the fact that he had a faucet installed in his abdomen to drain ill humors. Pynchon follows suit by converting Bongo-Shaftsbury to a mechanical doll. Esther Harvitz's nose job is graphically described literally blow by blow as Schoenmaker's assistant, Trench, enthralls himself with the sexual implications of injections of anesthetic. During the operation Esther realizes her latent desire for oblivion: "It was almost a mystic experience . . . where the highest condition we can attain is that of an object—a rock. It was like that; I felt myself drifting down, this delicious loss of Estherhood, becoming more and more a blob, with no worries, traumas, nothing: only Being" (106). Captivated by the experience, Esther becomes Schoenmaker's lover, while he schemes to remake her completely into his ideal image.

While the decadence of the Whole Sick Crew may be taken as low comedy, the implications of entropic drift and the extension of prosthetics into a mode of living are most frighteningly realized in the later incarnations of V. As Vera Meroving she acquires a glass eye with an iris in the shape of a clock. By the time she is destroyed by the Maltese children in a parody of crucifixion, she must be literally dismantled. Fausto Maijstral watches as the children remove her artificial eye, the star sapphire in her navel, and her false teeth, and wonders: "Surely her arms and breasts could be detached; the skin of her legs be peeled away to reveal some intricate understructure of silver openwork. Perhaps the trunk itself contained other wonders: intestines of parti-coloured silk, gay balloon-lungs, a rococo heart" (343). Stencil's daydream of her at age seventy-six extends the horror of this vision:

skin radiant with the bloom of some new plastic; both eyes glass but now containing photoelectric cells, connected by silver electrodes to optic nerves of purest copper wire and leading to a brain exquisitely wrought as a diode matrix could ever be. Solenoid relays would be her ganglia, servo-actuators move her flawless nylon limbs, hydraulic fluid be sent by a platinum heart-pump through butyrate veins and arteries. . . . Even a complex system of pressure transducers located in a marvelous vagina of polyethylene; the variable arms of their Wheatstone bridges all leading to a single silver cable which fed pleasure-voltages direct to the correct register of the digital machine in her skull. And whenever she smiled or grinned in ecstasy there would gleam her crowning feature: Eigenvalue's precious dentures (411–12).

VISION AND ANTI-VISION IN *V.*

V.'s transformations from Victoria Wren to the
Bad Priest signify a parody of religious metamorphoses in their tendency toward the inanimate. As Victoria, V. acquires the name of the queen, the practitioner
of divisive colonialism. As Veronica Manganese she
combines the name of a saint with that of a chemically
active metal that does not occur free in nature. As
Vera Meroving she is truth and the name of a dynasty
noted for war. She is also Virginia, Venezuela, Vesuvius,
Valetta, Vheissu, Venus, V1 and V2 rockets, Machi-
avellian *virtu*, the V of a woman's spread thighs; a per-
vasive mixture of womb and tomb, love and death,
hothouse and street. By embodying all, she represents
the entropic force that removes distinctions, a Thanatos drive that produces sterile sameness. Thus, on
Malta, "the hub of fortune's wheel," "manhood . . .
became increasingly defined in terms of rockhood"
(325) as the Bad Priest counsels young girls to "avoid
the sensual extremes—pleasure of intercourse, pain of
childbirth"—and young boys "to find strength in—
and be like—the rock of their island" (340).

In rendering the act of love a narcissistic fetish, V.
substitutes voyeurism for communication. Self-indul-
gent fantasy replaces interaction and eradicates
growth and change. V. appears in Paris in 1913 at the
age of thirty-three (the age of Christ when crucified)
replete with the trappings of wealthy decadence and in
love with a fifteen-year-old dancer named Mélanie

(black) l'Heuremaudit (the cursed hour). Their love-making takes place through mirrors so that V., Mélanie, and the mirror image create a trinity in which "dominance and submission didn't apply; the pattern of three was symbiotic and mutual" (409–10). As an inert parody of the Paraclete, V. makes fetishism a totem and unites love and death: "Dead at last, they would be one with the inanimate universe and with each other. Love-play until then thus becomes an impersonation of the inanimate, a transvestism not between sexes but between quick and dead, human and fetish" (410). The relation of the W in womb to a double V acquires horrific connotations in this context. Pynchon converts primitive totems to modern obsessions in his depiction of a ballet performance reminiscent of the premiere of Stravinsky's *Rite of Spring*, during which a riot ensued. Mélanie is literally sacrificed in her role as a virgin who is to be impaled on a pole. Ironically, she fails to wear her protective device: "Adorned with so many combs, bracelets, sequins, she might have become confused in this fetish-world and neglected to add to herself the one inanimate object that would have saved her" (414).

The terrifying implications of narcissistic fetishism are most poignantly considered when V. appears as Vera Meroving in 1922 in German-occupied Southwest Africa. An uprising of the Bondelzwarts, a subdivision of the Hottentot tribe, against South African

VISION AND ANTI-VISION IN *V.*

rule is under way, and an enclave of Germans barricade themselves in Foppl's house and indulge in a marathon siege party. In this hothouse environment decadence prevails. The reader witnesses a microcosm of the attempts of modern man to eradicate the responsibilities that civilization imposes on him. Foppl kisses a portrait of General Lothar von Trotha, who exterminated over sixty thousand natives in 1904, glorifying von Trotha for permitting him to forget the lessons of history. Kurt Mondaugen recalls Foppl's praise:

It's impossible to describe the sudden release; the comfort, the luxury; when you knew you could safely forget all the rote-lessons you'd had to learn about the value and dignity of human life. I had the same feeling once in the Realgymnasium when they told us we wouldn't be responsible in the examination for all the historical dates we'd spent weeks memorizing (253).

The philosopher George Santayana warned that "those who cannot remember the past are condemned to repeat it."[8] The disturbing implications of this statement apply to *V.* as witnessed in the similarities between the outlooks of the Whole Sick Crew and those of the members of Foppl's siege party. Distinctions between the lackadaisical contemporary American and the vicious Nazi prototype begin to fade when the teachings of civilization are ignored.

Pynchon indicts colonialism, a subject that he will turn to at greater length in *Gravity's Rainbow*, as an attempt to eradicate the values of the natives and to transpose them into reflections of the obsessions of the occupiers. Franz Kafka stated that "every crime is preceded by a spiritual mutilation."[9] Lacking any spiritual or human dimension, the Germans seek to annihilate any reminder of the sacred and, through mass violence, to reduce their victims to their own inanimate level. Fleische experiences a revelation concerning this unity of victim and victimizer after brutally murdering one Hottentot rebel:

Things seemed all at once to fall into a pattern: a great cosmic fluttering in the blank, bright sky and each grain of sand, each cactus spine, each feather of the circling vulture above them and invisible molecule of heated air seemed to shift imperceptibly so that this black and he, and every other black he would henceforth have to kill slid into alignment, assumed a set symmetry. . . . It had only to do with the destroyer and the destroyed, and the act which united them (264).

As a foreshadowing of the Nazi holocaust, Fleische's attitude merges with that of all colonizers who must protect their interests by assimilating or annihilating deviant points of view. In this respect Pynchon views the horrors enacted by the Germans in Southwest Africa, reminiscent of those engendered by Kurtz in Joseph Conrad's *Heart of Darkness*, as a logical extension of the capitulation to the void which V. personifies and to which twentieth-century life has succumbed.

Tourism serves as a motif that extends the colonial theme. The tourist possesses the colonial mentality in being unwilling to see the land on which he is trespassing from the natives' perspective. Instead, he chooses to interpret his experience from a familiar and self-contained viewpoint which differs very little from that of other tourists. The Baedeker guidebook dictates what he sees and how he sees it, rendering travel a solipsistic rather than a broadening experience. Pynchon invites us to compare the tourist philosophy of forcing reality to conform to illusion with other quests for inanimate sameness. In V.'s voyeuristic affair with Mélanie, for example; "their love was in its way only another version of tourism; for as tourists bring into the world as it has evolved part of another, and eventually create a parallel society of their own in every city, so the Kingdom of Death is served by fetish-constructions like V.'s, which represent a kind of infiltration" (411). Schoenmaker's desire to remake Esther, the Germans' brutal attempts to suppress the Hottentots, and V.'s prosthetic conversions present equivalent examples. The third chapter of *V.*, a revision of "Under the Rose," is set during the Fashoda crisis in

Cairo and presents eight sections narrated by Egyptians observing European tourists indulging in their Baedeker illusions. Pynchon complicates and comments on the illusions that these tourists impose by having the Egyptians in turn fantasize roles and situations for them during the course of their narration. Disguise is unmasked through disguise. However, any revelations remain problematic when the reader considers that the entire chapter is filtered through the point of view of Stencil, "a quick-change artist" who "does eight impersonations" of events that occurred when he was not alive. Pynchon's narrative legerdemain thus explodes the concept of a reliable point of view in the context of exposing the limited vision inherent in tourism.

In his depiction of the social misfits of 1950s America and the idea of yo-yoing as travel for its own sake, Pynchon is clearly influenced by Jack Kerouac's *On the Road*, a novel that was at the height of its popularity during the period that he came of age. In many respects *V.* fits the picaresque genre as a satirical road novel during the course of which neither protagonist undergoes any significant alteration in character. Stencil perpetuates himself through the perpetuation of his quest for V., manufacturing illusions to extend the inertia of his reductive world view. Profane's last words are "offhand I'd say I haven't learned a goddam thing" (454), and he leaves the novel hand in hand

with Brenda Wigglesworth, who owns seventy-two
pairs of Bermuda shorts, writes phony college-girl
poems, and is at the conclusion of her Grand Tour.
The basic epistemological quest that is at the center of
the experience of reading is tinged with doubt by en-
trusting interpretation to Stencil and Profane. The
reader himself becomes a tourist through a collection
of words, his Baedeker guide an exercise in narrative
point of view. In the case of *V.*, his experience of the
past is stencilized and his communion with the present
is profaned.

The narrator of Nabokov's *The Real Life of Se-
bastian Knight* (1941) is also named V (presumably
Vladimir). While engaged in a posthumous investigation of his half-brother's secret life, he discovers that
his half-brother's last lover had assumed several identities. Toward the conclusion of the book V confesses
that his search had been nothing more than a conjurer's show. The similarity of structure and intent between Nabokov's novel and that of his student,
Pynchon, is particularly interesting given *V.*'s insistence on the narrator as conjurer and on the void to
which the quest for vision frequently leads. Most of
the characters in *V.* play the role of the tourist in living
their lives, choosing surface impressions that preserve
preprogrammed conceptions rather than penetrating
beneath the surface into the unexplored and disrup-
tive. As Stencil conjures the murder of one of his

father's colleagues, Porpentine, during his last impersonation in chapter 3, the reader is never told who he
is impersonating, who is watching the spy drama that
unfolds. While the lack of a specific identity on which
to attach point of view foreshadows an equivalent oc-
currence in the epilogue, Pynchon injects irony when
the same unidentified narrator offers a central thematic
statement as Porpentine dies: "Vision must be the last
to go. There must also be a nearly imperceptible line
between an eye that reflects and an eye that receives"
(94). Either Pynchon intrudes here to lend authorial
authority to this sage comment or he remains, like the
artist of Flaubert and Joyce, refined out of existence.
The reader can never be certain, but in a relentless
quest to make sense of the book and of the world, one
must grapple with the statement. As long as the reader
maintains an awareness that what he grapples with is
a construct, a fiction; as long as he reads with a
healthy paranoia, he can sustain the "nearly imperceptible line" and avoid the solipsistic trap.

In a novel so concerned with questions of identity
and disguise and with the distinctions between perception and fetish, Pynchon also concerns himself with
the fine line that may be drawn between instructive
and destructive knowledge. Vera Meroving's artificial
left eye is but one immediate symbol of degeneracy
into an inanimate vision, of an eye that reflects but
does not receive; the vision of colonial oppression, of

VISION AND ANTI-VISION IN *V.*

Baedeker repetition. To only receive information without imposing any constructs upon it is to engage in the entropic drift of the Whole Sick Crew. In some instances, V. is so horrifying because she is so compelling and because she haunts both the inhabited land and the realm beneath it. Fairing's parish is one example of this. Vheissu is another. The quest for vision, for meaning beyond the repetitive sameness that V. has brought to modern life, leads Hugh Godolphin into the rainbow mockery that lines the annihilative void of V's lair.

Godolphin confesses his story of Vheissu to Victoria Wren in Florence in 1899. Victoria is no longer a devout Catholic considering the prospect of becoming a nun but unwilling to compete for the Son of God with a "great harem clad in black," as she was in Cairo the previous year. Now "self-proclaimed a citizen of the world" (166), she experiences an epiphany of the merger of Dynamo and Virgin during the riots at the Venezuelan consulate: "It was as if she saw herself embodying a female principle, acting as complement to all this bursting, explosive male energy" (209). A land of shimmering colors and iridescent spider monkeys "as if you lived inside a madman's kaleidoscope," Vheissu also contains "barbarity, insurrection, internecine feud" (170). Godolphin, an English explorer, discovers this remote land and is subsequently haunted by it until he completes his expedition with a journey to the South Pole. There he discovers a spider monkey's frozen carcass buried by the inhabitants of Vheissu who have followed him since he left their country, and experiences the nihilistic vision that it signifies: "a mockery of life, planted where everything but Hugh Godolphin was inanimate. . . . The skin which had wrinkled through my nightmares was all there had ever been. Vheissu itself, a gaudy dream. Of what the Antarctic in this world is closest to: a dream of annihilation" (206).

The story of Vheissu might have been lifted from the conclusion of Poe's *The Narrative of Arthur Gordon Pym*.[10] The protagonist of Poe's novel confirms the Symmes theory that there existed a passage to the earth's core by reaching the dreamlike, milky seascape at the South Pole that is the portal to the center of the earth. Godolphin's discovery of the nothingness that underlies the disguise of the surface, however, negates rather than confirms. In Florence, Vheissu is the subject of international intrigue. It is suspected by some to be Vesuvius and by others to be Venezuela. Another version holds that the natives of Vheissu intend to infiltrate the rest of the world through underground tunnels. Common to all these suspicions is the connection of Vheissu with an apocalyptic force, the negation beneath the surface of multiplicity.

The riot at the Venezuelan consulate occurs at the same time that Rafael Mantissa, a friend of Godolphin's, is carrying out his plot to steal Botticelli's *Birth of Venus* from the Uffizi gallery. Victoria Wren's epiphany, her transformation to V. the anti-Venus, is simultaneous with Mantissa's revelation as his accomplice cuts the Botticelli canvas from its frame. Mantissa's name derives from *mantis,* which is Greek for seer,[11] and he serves a function similar to that of Tiresias in Eliot's "The Waste Land." His vision is prompted by Godolphin's tale of Vheissu. Suddenly glimpsing the emptiness behind the painting's captivating surface, he abandons his larcenous intentions. Mantissa understands that his fascination with the painting is no different than Godolphin's obsession with Vheissu that "isolated [him] from a human community" (184), that a relationship with such a demanding mistress would obliterate all other concerns. Through absolutism, obsession, a conversion to a hothouse environment, Venus the creative life force becomes V. the agent of decay. Unlike Godolphin and unlike Herbert Stencil, Mantissa says no to the alluring surface and to the void beneath it and thereby preserves himself.

Vision and anti-vision converge in Kurt Mondaugen's search for meaning in sferics (atmospheric disturbances that accompany radio transmissions). Like the quest for Vheissu and V., Mondaugen's attempt to find messages embedded in random atmospheric radio disturbances becomes an obsessive fetish. Eventually Vera Meroving's lover, a sadistic transvestite named

UNDERSTANDING THOMAS PYNCHON

Weissmann, who appears as Blicero in *Gravity's Rainbow*, breaks the code. By removing every third letter that Mondaugen has transcribed from the sferics, he obtains GODMEANTNUURK which rearranged spells Kurt Mondaugen. Mondaugen's search ends where it began; his data mock him. The remaining letters yield the first proposition of Ludwig Wittgenstein's *Tractatus*, "Die Welt ist alles was der Fall ist" (the world is all that the case is). Deterministic continuity is denied in a confirmation of Sidney Stencil's view of the Situation as having no objective reality. Given the primacy of accident, any connective plots become paranoid inventions. The answer is that there is no answer. Like Mondaugen's sferics, the meaning of V. has no objective reality. Pynchon's awareness of the use of *v* as a symbol for "variant reading" and for the logical relationship "or" underscores this implication. The settings for the six historical chapters have no linear relationship. The common links are the destruction in the foreground and the haunting presence of V. However, the references to V. are all supplied by the dubious Stencil, and her symbolic qualities are inferred by the reader who, like Mondaugen, is mocked by what he reads.

As a foil to the religious parody that V. exhibits, Paola Maijstral emerges as a figure of salvation. Robert Graves's *The White Goddess*, to which Pynchon specifically alludes (61), calls for the reestablishment of a humanistic mythology to reverse the technological corruption of the modern world. By investing Paola with the qualities of the White Goddess, a trifold goddess of Aegean beginnings who presides over birth, love, and death, Pynchon offers an alternative to the death wish fostered by V. With the crucifixion of the Bad Priest, the final incarnation of V. in the novel, *V.* presents the possibility of a rebirth of humanistic myth through Paola.

Faith in any possibility of a conversion from the void to the animate is invested in Paola, whom we first encounter as a barmaid named Beatrice (as are all the barmaids) at the Sailor's Grave on Christmas Eve. In the *Divine Comedy*, Beatrice is the idealization of wisdom through faith who guides Dante through Paradise. In V., Paola has left her husband, Pappy Hod, and is undergoing a protean quest for a sense of unity and peace. She tells Profane, "Isn't that what we all want, Benny? Just a little peace. Nobody jumping out and biting you on the ass" (16).

Paola's relationship to the Paraclete, a transcendent and unifying figure in the Trinity, is immediately hinted at: "She could be any age she wanted. And you suspected any nationality, for Paola knew scraps it seemed of all tongues" (14). The idea of tongues is a recurring motif in *V.*[12] In a bierhalle early in the book the reader encounters a "triangular stain [which] swam somewhere over the crown, like a tongue on Pentecost" (92). We later see the Bad Priest speaking in tongues at her crucifixion. The significance becomes more apparent upon referring to Acts 2:1–4: "And when the day of Pentecost was fully come, they were all with one accord in one place. And suddenly there came a sound from heaven, as of a rushing mighty wind, and it filled all the house where they were sitting. And there appeared unto them cloven tongues, like as of fire, and it sat upon each of them. And they were all filled with the Holy Ghost, and began to speak with other tongues, as the Spirit gave them utterance." This Pentecostal wind is reflected in Paola's last name, Maijstral, which is a Maltese wind. Furthermore, it is a wind that blows once every three days, thus underscoring the relation to the Trinity.

V.'s descent into the realm of the inanimate is mirrored in Paola's ascent into the realm of human relations: "The girl lived proper nouns. Persons, places. No things. Had anyone told her about things?" (51). The Bad Priest had convinced Paola's mother, Elena, to have an abortion, but is foiled when Elena meets Father Avalanche. As an opposing force to the Bad Priest, Father Avalanche is referred to as A, an inverted V, in Fausto Maijstral's journal. His name also indicates his capacity to dispel the rockhood that the Bad Priest urges on the Maltese. As Victoria Wren, V. whimsically obtains an ivory comb, the teeth of which are in the shape of five crucified British soldiers (V is, of course, the Roman numeral for five). Graves writes of an ivory comb as an accessory of the White Goddess,[13] and the comb is restored to its rightful owner when it is passed to Paola during the dismantling of the Bad Priest.

According to legend the apostle Paul was shipwrecked in A.D. 60 on Malta, where he converted the inhabitants to Christianity. Paola is Italian for Paul, and it is her own conversion to the role of Paraclete that offers the possibility for recovery from the inertia that has been sustained since the crucifixion of the Bad Priest. Like V., Paola undergoes several transformations during the course of the novel, including that of the black prostitute, Ruby, which permits her to acquire McClintic Sphere's "keep cool, but care" philosophy. Her capacity to love permits a temperance that resolves the polarity of indifference versus fanaticism prospering in V.'s realm. In caring, she also represents the literal translation of *Paraclete*—comforter.

Fausto perceives the need for unity through myth, for a "resurgence of humanity in the automaton, health in the decadent" (337). On Malta the Dynamo and the Virgin, sex and death, conjoin. Between 1940 and 1943 the island was subjected to over two thousand heavy air raids by Italian and German planes, but the solid fortifications and air-raid shelters built into the rock kept the Axis powers from bombing Malta into surrender. Fausto takes refuge in the sewers from the incessant bombings that have killed his wife and invests the matriarchal island with human qualities:[14] "Malta is a noun feminine and proper. Italians have indeed been attempting her defloration since the 8th of June. She lies on her back in the sea, sullen; an immemorial woman. Spread to the explosive orgasms of Mussolini bombs" (318). Whereas Profane failed to gain knowledge from his experience in the sewer and Fairing went insane, Fausto, by immersing himself in the metaphor of Malta, is able to emerge from his period of incubation capable of presiding over the death of the Bad Priest as a priest himself and of allowing her death to take place through "a sin of omission" (345). In his classic study of an archetype, *The Great Mother*, Erich Neumann refers specifically to this archetypal situation in Malta: "We have repeatedly referred to the spiritual aspect of the feminine transformative character, which leads through suffering and death, sacrifice and annihilation, to renewal, rebirth, and immortality. But such transformation is possible only when what is to be transformed enters wholly into the Feminine principle. . . . as in Malta long before the days of healing in the Greek shrines of Asclepius, the sick man undergoes a slumber of 'incubation,' in the course of which he encounters the healing godhead."[15]

Fausto's transformations project onto those of Paola. His prayer for her heralds her eventual grasp of a unity that exists beyond the "Great Lie," a unity that depends on a resurgence of humanity for its existence: "May you be only Paola, one girl: a single given heart, a whole mind at peace" (314). Fausto emerges as a modified John the Baptist figure who does not proclaim but quietly hopes for the possibility of a whole person to issue from the rubble of the cellar in which the Bad Priest lies and from the ashes of his world.[16]

In his own priestly preparation of the Bad Priest for death, Fausto symbolically confirms the transition from the realm of the inanimate to the realm of the animate. Instead of using oil from a chalice to anoint her sense organs, he dips blood from her navel. Out of the wound, caused by the children's removal of the inert star sapphire, comes the latent healing impulse that marks the return from the province of the plastic to the dominion of the human. However, a Pynchon novel—or, for that matter, any postmodern novel—cannot be modeled on a Dr. Jekyll and Mr. Hyde, good versus evil, duality. In the age of uncertainty and relativity the discrete personalities and definitive values found in Victorian novels are rendered mutable. As D. H. Lawrence stated in his essay "Morality and the Novel," when we "try to nail anything down, . . . the novel gets up and walks away with the nail."[17] In *V.* clues dissipate as they coalesce and, as Tony Tanner writes, "Reconstruction is also deconstruction."[18]

Fausto goes through a sequence of identities and continually comments on what he has previously written. He learns that life's single lesson is "that there is more accident to it than a man can ever admit to in a lifetime and stay sane" (320–21). It is therefore the role of the poet in the twentieth century to lie. Metaphor-making becomes a necessary misology, an assumption of a disguise that creates a momentary stay against confusion. By investing objects with human qualities, the poet creates a temporary illusion that combats the conversion of humans to rockhood and thereby enables civilization to continue. For the children of Malta, for example, "the R.A.F. game was [a] metaphor they devised to veil the world that was. . . . It was poetry in a vacuum" (331–32). The corollary quandary to this act is that identity is linked to an arbitrary metaphor, an artifice, that must be continually freshened to preserve the vitality of that identity. To rest in an illusion is to permit the intrusion of the inanimate, to succumb to the seduction of V. Thus Pynchon reminds his reader that the reality of the novel, like that of the world, is a fiction.

By selecting occurrences in the history of various countries at different times over the past century, Pynchon dangles the causal carrot before his reader. At the same time he uses his protagonists to parody the reader's attempts at concrete connections. Plots, *V.* suggests, are human inventions, a weaving together of accidental resemblances. Empirical quests are actually myopic yo-yoings through the chaos of time. Imagi-

VISION AND ANTI-VISION IN *V.*

nary constructs offer reprieves from the void, but must themselves be constantly renewed. However, the reader's active engagement with the text also becomes a creative act that transforms and renews. One's willingness to interpret while accepting the limitations of interpretation presents a version of the "keep cool, but care" philosophy that it is imperative to maintain as a defense against creative exhaustion.

The contradictory strands and signals that permeate *V.* are not mutually exclusive, nor do they necessarily constitute a dialectic. Instead, the reader is forced to participate in an inclusive dynamic that resists solidity and forces a continual rearrangement of perspective. The novel and every chapter in the novel conclude inconclusively. Part of Pynchon's appeal has to do with his depiction of the limits of rationalism and of the negative consequences of the overreliance on empiricism in the western world view. The colonial mania to determine absolute hierarchies by which to judge the value of other human beings is but one extension of the process of assigning concepts to rigid compartments that the rational tradition fosters. Pynchon is difficult because he undermines the very methods through which we normally approach understanding. He accuses them of being stale and destructive and, through the experience of coming to terms with his novel, asks us to revitalize our lives through new methods.

In the epilogue of the novel Mehemet, the master of the ship that is caught in the waterspout off Malta in which Sidney Stencil is drowned, serves as another Tiresias figure. He sails with the ancient goddess of sexual love, Astarte, as his figurehead and narrates the story of the Maltese witch, Mara (a forerunner of V.?), to Stencil. A true anachronism, Mehemet slipped through a rift in time during 1324 to find himself displaced into the modern world. He rejects Stencil's reductive rationalizations regarding old age, calling them attempts "to bring it down to a size you can look at and feel comfortable." "The only change is toward death," he cheerfully states with complete acceptance (460). Mehemet, the time-traveler, rejects linear and cyclical views of history. On Malta, "where all history seemed simultaneously present" (481), one can project whatever configurations one wishes into the spin of fortune's wheel; "the basic arrangement was constant; . . . The hub still held the spokes in place and the meeting-place of the spokes still defined the hub" (338). Pynchon asks his reader to recognize the constancy of the hub but, like the Maltese children, to push the wheel over from its vertical position so that it is "dead-level, its own rim only that of the sea's horizon" (339). Then he can extend himself beyond the repetitive confines of a single sphere of vision and create the metaphors that are a prerequisite for survival.

VISION AND ANTI-VISION IN *V.*

Notes

1. Frank D. McConnell, *Four Postwar American Novelists* (Chicago: University of Chicago Press, 1977) 167.

2. Robert D. Newman, "The White Goddess Restored: Affirmation in Pynchon's *V.*," *University of Mississippi Studies in English* 4 (1983): 178–86. An earlier version of the section of this chapter concerning Paola Maijstral first appeared in this essay.

3. Thomas Pynchon, *V.* (Philadelphia: Lippincott, 1963) 461. Further references will be noted parenthetically.

4. David Cowart, *Thomas Pynchon: The Art of Allusion* (Carbondale: Southern Illinois University Press, 1980) 18.

5. Norbert Wiener, *The Human Use of Human Beings: Cybernetics and Society* (New York: Avon, 1967) 38–39.

6. Wiener, 260–61. In his excellent essay "Caries and Cabals," Tony Tanner discusses the relevance of Wiener's discussion of Manicheanism to *V.* (*City of Words: American Fiction 1950–1970* [New York: Harper, 1971]).

7. Roger B. Henkle, "Pynchon's Tapestries on the Western Wall," *Modern Fiction Studies* 17, 2 (1971): 212.

8. George Santayana, *Reason in Common Sense* (New York: Scribner's, 1905) 284.

9. Gustav Janouch, *Conversations with Kafka* (Frankfurt: Andre Deutsch, 1968) 50.

10. Hanjo Berressem, "Godolphin-Goodolphin-Goodol'phin-Good ol'Pyn-Good ol'Pym: A Question of Integration," *Pynchon Notes* 10 (Oct. 1982): 3–17.

11. Cowart 20.

12. W. T. Lhamon, Jr., "Pentecost, Promiscuity, and Pynchon's *V.:* From the Scaffold to the Impulsive," *Twentieth Century Literature* 21, 2 (1975), 163–76. Lhamon sees tongues functioning thematically in *V.* as representing the difference between entropy and Pentecost.

13. Robert Graves, *The White Goddess*, rev. ed. (New York: Farrar, Straus, 1959) 438ff.

14. The cult of the White Goddess is thought to have achieved its highest and most intricate form in Malta; See Jacquetta Hawkes and Leonard Woolley, *Prehistory and the Beginnings of Civilization* (New York: Allen and Unwin, 1963) 338.

15. Erich Neumann, *The Great Mother* (Princeton: Princeton University Press, 1963) 291–92.

16. See Robert D. Newman, "Pynchon's Use of Carob in *V.*," *Notes on Contemporary Literature* 9 (1981): 11, for further discussion of Fausto as a John the Baptist figure.

17. D. H. Lawrence, *Phoenix* (New York: Penguin, 1980) 528.

18. Tony Tanner, *Thomas Pynchon* (New York: Methuen, 1982) 47.

CHAPTER FOUR

The Quest for Metaphor in *The Crying of Lot 49*

At the end of his introduction to *Slow Learner*, after discussing "The Secret Integration" as an indication of his authorial evolution, Pynchon comments: "As is clear from the up-and-down shape of my learning curve, however, it was too much to expect that I'd keep on for long in this positive or professional direction. The next story I wrote was 'The Crying of Lot 49,' which was marketed as a 'novel,' and in which I seem to have forgotten most of what I thought I'd learned up till then." As usual, it is difficult to know just how to take Pynchon. Certainly literary critics, at least those initially inclined to appreciate Pynchon, seem to welcome *The Crying of Lot 49*—whether novel, novella, or story—as a compact, unified work that distills many of the issues encountered in the more diffuse and convoluted *V.* and *Gravity's Rainbow*. Numerous general essays on Pynchon choose to light upon *Lot 49* rather than the other novels in order to demonstrate their assertions, and instructors of

contemporary literature courses choose it as an introduction to the intricacies of Pynchon's works. Counter-
culture enthusiasts too regard it as one of the
quintessential books reflecting the "sixties experience."
Regardless of Pynchon's self-deprecating assessment,
Lot 49 is not a lapse in the author's growth as a writer,
nor should it be regarded only as a coda to *V.* or as a
precursor of *Gravity's Rainbow.* The book stands on
its own as a commentary on American culture and as
an investigation into the uses and misuses of metaphor.

Like *V.*, *The Crying of Lot 49*, published in 1966,
concerns a quest, the object of which becomes increasingly unclear as the novel progresses.[1] Entropy, paranoia, and revelation still recur as themes, and bizarre
comedy again complements the novel's tragic implications while simultaneously diverting attention from
them. Pynchon defuses our reliance on logic and dialectic while rendering ambiguous the possibility of
acausal leaps of knowledge. Theme and plot are organized around dualities, yet the very notion of duality
as a means for interpreting experience is undermined
during the course of the novel. However, a network of
connections proliferates within the point of view of
the protagonist, with whom, despite her expressions
of self-doubt and the narrative flippancy that often accompanies them, the reader inevitably identifies.

THE CRYING OF LOT 49

The novel begins, appropriately, with contradictions:

One summer afternoon Mrs Oedipa Maas came home from a Tupperware party whose hostess had put perhaps too much kirsch in the fondue to find that she, Oedipa, had been named executor, or she supposed executrix, of the estate of one Pierce Inverarity, a California real estate mogul who had once lost two million dollars in his spare time but still had assets numerous and tangled enough to make the job of sorting it all out more than honorary.[2]

Twice in the first sentence the reader encounters the character's name, which generates mythological, Freudian, and generally symbolic associations that are simultaneously deflated by the ordinariness of her suburban existence. Oedipa's role as a questing heroine is also parodied since her quest is merely to execute the estate of Pierce Inverarity, her former lover. What the reader does not yet understand is the degree to which Oedipa's "job of sorting it all out" also becomes the reader's quest to come to terms with the novel and with his or her culture.

As Oedipa ventures into the tangled dimensions of Inverarity's holdings, she discovers that they are boundless, that in fact Pierce's "legacy was America" (178). Furthermore, it is an America whose dreams have been bankrupted by the industrial sameness that Pierce has fomented, causing it to fall into an endless replication of tired concepts. The pioneering spirit of individualism and inventiveness has given way to conglomerates like Yoyodyne, of which Pierce is a "founding father" (26), that subsume originality and initiative under a suffocating cloak of self-perpetuation. Stanley Koteks, an employee of Yoyodyne, complains to Oedipa that the corporation assumes all patents of its employees' inventions, hence removing any incentive for creativity. This spirit seems to infuse the culture as a whole.

Just as Yoyodyne's offices are a stultifying nightmare of order and sameness, San Narciso, an obvious play on the Narcissus myth, is "like many named places in California . . . less an identifiable city than a grouping of concepts—census tracts, special purpose bond-issue districts, shopping nuclei, all overlaid with access roads to its own freeway" (24). As Oedipa peers into the valley at the rows and rows of repetitive houses, she thinks of the time she had seen her first printed circuit. Earlier she reflected upon how identical all her days seem after a typical day of shopping and gardening, preparing her batch of whiskey sours, and awaiting the arrival of her husband, Mucho Maas, from work. To her husband's frustration at his sense of meaninglessness, she replies, "You're too sensitive" (12), a term that will attain further levels of meaning as the novel progresses.

THE CRYING OF LOT 49

Pierce Inverarity's America has trapped its constituents, who either passively accept a dull aimlessness or frantically react against it; but both responses undermine any sense of direction or control. Mucho Maas, perceiving the cultural stagnation brought about by the mechanization of human beings, quits his job as a used car salesman. The National Automobile Dealers' Association is, for him, too reminiscent of its acronym—NADA. For Mucho, who "doesn't believe any of it," the best way to drown out his sordid social vision is with the noise that he generates as a disk jockey for KCUF (which reversed exemplifies the juvenile humor purposely undermining the serious tone of much of the novel). Oedipa's therapist, Dr. Hilarius, who reminds Oedipa of portraits of Uncle Sam, has taken to self-deluding voyages on LSD in which he tries to involve other suburban housewives under the guise of scientific experimentation. Oedipa's lawyer, Roseman, is obsessed with his inferiority to Perry Mason, and devotes his energy to a manuscript entitled "The Profession v. Perry Mason." His attempts to play footsie under the table with Oedipa are frustrated by the boots she wears. Typically, she "couldn't feel much of anything" (19).

Oedipa's situation, and by implication the situation of America, is epitomized in the scene that concludes chapter 1. Here Oedipa reflects upon a painting by Remedios Varo she had seen in Mexico City during her affair with Pierce. Before the affair "there had hung the sense of buffering, insulation, she had noticed the absence of an intensity, as if watching a movie, just perceptibly out of focus, that the projectionist refused to fix" (20). Identifying with Rapunzel, Oedipa wants to let down her hair from the tower confining her, and longs to be rescued by some knight of deliverance. Until she saw the painting, she felt that Pierce was that knight:

In the central painting of a triptych, titled "Bordando el Manto Terrestre," were a number of frail girls with heart-shaped faces, huge eyes, spun-gold hair, prisoners in the top room of a circular tower, embroidering a kind of tapestry which spilled out the slit windows and into a void, seeking hopelessly to fill the void: for all the other buildings and creatures, all the waves, ships and forests of the earth were contained in this tapestry, and the tapestry was the world (21).

This passage and Oedipa's subsequent reactions to it determine the dimensions of *The Crying of Lot 49*. Oedipa realizes that she has been playacting within a self-conceived fairy tale that has fostered the illusion of escape when indeed the tower has contributed to her isolation. Her choices appear to be either solipsism or assimilation, both of which are dead ends. With assimilation into the void outside the tower comes the loss of identity, the anonymity of invention prevalent at Yoyodyne, the lack of diversity of America, the

THE CRYING OF LOT 49

danger of disintegration. With the solipsism of the tower comes the danger of madness reflected in Hilarius's fantasy world. One can choose a totally external or a totally internal life, accept victimization by the system or guard against it by retreating into paranoia. Against this either/or construct as backdrop, Oedipa begins her heroic quest to "project a world" (82), to find meaning through metaphor.

As several critics have noted, *Lot 49* employs the inverse relationship between entropy as a concept in thermodynamic theory and in information theory and applies it to a cultural context.[3] In thermodynamic theory entropy refers to the degree of disorganization of molecules within a closed system, a uniform randomness that allows for no differentiation among the parts of a system. Hence maximum entropy yields a chaos of sameness. In information theory the implications are positive rather than negative, for disorganization increases the potential information that may be conveyed. Maximum entropy in this respect produces a chaos of multiplicity.

At the beginning of the novel Oedipa's conventionality and the lifeless repetition the reader encounters in the traces of American culture suggest an entropic system in the thermodynamic sense. However, the estate that Inverarity leaves Oedipa to sort out yields more and more information about that system as *Lot 49* progresses, to the point that its diversity becomes bewildering. At the end of chapter 1 Oedipa despairs when she assesses her life as trapped in entropic drift. The more information she gains concerning Tristero, however, the more her choices proliferate beyond the limited binary alternatives of assimilation or solipsism, thus offsetting personal and, potentially, cultural entropy. At the beginning of chapter 4, for example, Oedipa begins to feel the pressure of "revelations which now seemed to come crowding in exponentially, as if the more she collected the more would come to her, until everything she saw, smelled, dreamed, remembered, would somehow come to be woven into The Tristero" (81). In addition to the fact that entropy in information theory does increase exponentially, a fact that lends some degree of objective truth to Oedipa's experience, Pynchon's use of the term *revelations* is important to the thematic texture of the novel.

Religious imagery frames the novel. Oedipa's first utterance is "the name of God" (9), and *Lot 49* concludes with the auctioneer spreading his arms "in a gesture that seemed to belong to the priesthood of some remote culture; perhaps to a descending angel" (183) as Oedipa awaits a revelation. Religious designs increasingly permeate Oedipa's perceptions of what is going on around her. In her initial view of San Narciso, which led her to equate the landscape with a printed circuit, the narrator tells us that "a revelation

also trembled just past the threshold of her understanding. . . . She and the Chevy seemed parked at
the centre of an odd, religious instant" (24). The appearance of the Tristero symbol of the muted post
horn on a stamp is considered "a sign" (115). The performance of *The Courier's Tragedy* that Oedipa attends concludes its fourth act with the "revelation" of
what really happened to the Lost Guard of Faggio, a
"miracle" in the presence of which "all fall to their
knees [and] bless the name of God" (74). The last word
of the act is "Trystero," which Oedipa later discovers
is the result of the director, Randolph Driblette, having introduced a textual variation which in turn was
the product of a pornographic corruption by the
Scurvhamites of the original text. The Scurvhamites,
she learns, were a seventeenth-century Puritan sect
devoted to the Word that attempted to damn the theater by tampering with its words. Their belief in a mechanical universe that is running down into
annihilation foreshadows the contemporary results of
the Calvinist approach to enterprise, an industrial society fallen into inertia and homogeneity. Pierce, a
prime mover of this cultural decay, is himself a type of
profane Peter (the name derives from *petrus*, meaning
rock) whose perverse church is a secular conglomerate
that utters hymns of greed in a resonant monotone,
thus inhibiting any meaningful communication. To Je-
sus Arrabal, the Mexican anarchist, Pierce is a "mir-

acle . . . another world's intrusion into this one" in that "he is too exactly and without a flaw the thing we fight, . . . as terrifying to me as a Virgin appearing to an Indian" (120).

Pierce's America has secularized communication so that little meaningful communion between individuals occurs. A morass of technological conveniences for disseminating information pervades the novel, yet the volume of information they generate does not compensate for the lack of diversity. Mr. Thoth, named for the Egyptian god of scribes, resides in a nursing home and, like the state of the written word, decays. He refers to TV as a "filthy machine" (91). When Oedipa enters Nefastis's home, cartoons blare from the TV, and Nefastis later invites her to have sex with him while they watch the news. When the paranoid Hilarius, believing that his role in the Gestapo may have been discovered, goes on a shooting spree, the TV crews that converge on Hilarius's office plead with Oedipa to keep him occupied so that they can get some footage. Rather than directly participating in life, the media become vehicles for voyeurism, generating both assimilation and solipsism because they replace human interaction. Driblette complains, "The words, who cares? . . . The reality is in *this* head. Mine. I'm the projector at the planetarium" (79). He eventually commits suicide by walking into the sea in his Gennaro costume, to the end acting a role that is exclusively self-referential. Most of the characters that populate *Lot 49* reflect the tragic irony wrought by the technological culture on the people who mindlessly perpetuate that culture. As the technological means for generating information accelerates, people seem to increasingly insulate themselves from interpersonal communication and to limit their sense of their own identities so as to become extensions of machinery. Oedipa, however, refuses to circumscribe her quest.

If Oedipa's espistemological quest structures the novel, the strip Botticelli scene in chapter 2 serves as a paradigm of its design (Botticelli is a word game, played somewhat like Twenty Questions). That Metzger, formerly child film star Baby Igor, is an actor turned lawyer while his cohort, Manny DiPresso, is a lawyer turned actor suggests that jobs have become mere playacting, a series of interchangeable roles the distinctions of which are only superficial. Again television offers a medium for random information upon which Oedipa must impose patterns. The Fangoso Lagoons commercial reminds her of her view of San Narciso as a printed circuit, and she conceives of the connection as "some promise of hierophany" (31). She perceives life as a foreordained conspiracy, a perception that acquires support when *Cashiered,* a film starring Baby Igor, appears on the TV. Even the can of hair spray that rockets around the bathroom knows "where it was going, she sensed" (37). Metzger offers

Oedipa clues to the film's ending in exchange for her removal of one item of clothing per clue. Typically, Oedipa insulates herself with several layers of clothing. Though the film is "one of endless repetitions" (34), entropy attacks as the reels get reversed. As a rock group named the Paranoids serenades them, Metzger eventually divests Oedipa of her clothes without revealing the ending of the film, although she falls asleep as he builds towards his sexual crescendo. Their eventual mutual climax coincides with that of the Paranoids whose profusion of electric guitars blows a fuse in Oedipa's room.

Strip Botticelli becomes a metaphor for the unmasking quest pattern of the book as Pynchon incorporates the preponderance of Heisenberg's uncertainty principle in twentieth-century physics to sound the death knell of epistemological certainty. Oedipa must battle entropy to make sense of all the clues she discovers, yet those clues both contribute information that aids her and complicate any resolution with their multiplicity. The novel's detective-story pattern is inverted, the clues not providing a solution to the protagonist's search but instead multiplying alternatives while rendering fixation on one of them a paranoid endeavor. The reader's attempts at sense-making are likewise confused, since the narrative voice undermines any stability of tone with jokes and juvenile comedy. Like Oedipa, the reader is teased into playing an intricate game, one in which his or her inevitable ordering of information is rendered potentially fallacious by a new series of apparently coherent clues. However, once the reader begins to arrange these clues into a system, still more information renders his or her system dubious while never completely eradicating its premises. Oedipa's quest for the meaning of Tristero is, like her attendance of *The Courier's Tragedy* and the reader's reading of *Lot 49*, a participation in a theatrical performance, in this case a striptease:

As if the breakaway gowns, net bras, jeweled garters and G-strings of historical configuration that would fall away were layered dense as Oedipa's own street-clothes in that game with Metzger in front of the Baby Igor movie; as if a plunge toward dawn indefinite black hours long would indeed be necessary before The Tristero could be revealed in its terrible nakedness. Would its smile, then, be coy, and would it flirt away harmlessly backstage, say good night with a Bourbon Street bow and leave her in peace? Or would it instead, the dance ended, come back down the runway, its luminous stare locked to Oedipa's, smile gone malign and pitiless; bend to her alone among the desolate rows of seats and begin to speak words she never wanted to hear? (54)

In discovering the Tristero system's expansiveness Oedipa descends to the underworld of America and finds a network of exiles that offers alternatives to assimilation or solipsism, the binary choices characterizing San Narciso. Historically Tristero has waged a campaign against entropic sameness, pitching the focus of its activities against attempts to regulate the act of communication. By battling the Thurn and Taxis postal monopoly, Tristero injects new information into a decaying system. For its agents the act of communication is sacred, and has been blasphemed by the proliferation of technological devices that inhibit rather than ease meaningful connections between people. Reliance on mechanical devices rather than the power of the word has contributed to a mechanical approach to life, thereby prohibiting a secure teleological sense of the universe while grinding the chain of being into a scattering of metallic shards. Tristero confronts stagnation with protean patterns of rebellion, thereby creating diversity and opening the system to continuous change. Some groups, like the right-wing Peter Pinquid Society, rebel only for the sake of rebellion and, in reality, offer to substitute one closed system for another. The Peter Pinquid Society requires its members to use the alternative mail system once a week whether they have something to communicate or not. This produces messages that contain no real information. Tristero, on the other hand, creatively designs to frustrate stultifying patterns and

THE CRYING OF LOT 49

evince surprise. Oedipa's mental list of its parodies of postage stamps provides a good example:

In the 15¢ dark green from the 1893 Columbian Exposition Issue ("Columbus Announcing His Discovery"), the faces of three courtiers receiving the news at the right-hand side of the stamp, had been subtly altered to express uncontrollable fright. In the 3¢ Mothers of America Issue, put out on Mother's Day, 1934, the flowers to the lower left of Whistler's Mother had been replaced by Venus's-flytrap, belladonna, poison sumac and a few others Oedipa had never seen. In the 1947 Postage Stamp Centenary Issue, commemorating the great postal reform that had meant the beginning of the end for private carriers, the head of a Pony Express rider at the lower left was set at a disturbing angle unknown among the living. The deep violet 3¢ regular issue of 1954 had a faint, menacing smile on the face of the Statue of Liberty (174).

Oedipa's descent into the underworld of her culture is also a voyage of self-discovery that revivifies her mythic roots. The numerous references to Egyptian mythic materials in *Lot 49*—Thoth, the *Book of the Dead*, hieroglyphs—contribute an infrastructure that links Oedipa's quest with the soul's descent into the underworld as depicted in the *Egyptian Book of the Dead*. C. G. Jung's commentaries on the Tibetan

Book of the Dead are helpful here. Jung has referred to the time that the soul resides in the underworld as a "Bardo existence" which, coincidentally, usually occupies forty-nine days. In terms of its psychological analogue, Jung has discussed this period as a difficult journey through the unfamiliar territory of the unconscious during which one must confront the repressed aspects of the self.[4] When Oedipa initially discovers the muted post horn symbol of Tristero lurking among bathroom graffiti, she thinks of hieroglyphs while copying the symbol in her memo book (52). The hieroglyphs indicate another world view, one that seeks connections rather than the dualistic distinctions that dominate the western intellectual tradition. In learning to translate the hieroglyphs, Oedipa rediscovers metaphor as a means of making sense. Metaphor-making is an act of imaginative creation, one that asserts similarity or connection based on the recognition of some pattern. Ironically, Tristero both urges and denies interpretation, thereby preserving its inward mystery and supplying the sense-making structure necessary to connect the world with meaning. By translating the hieroglyphs of Tristero, Oedipa realizes her obsession with "bringing something of herself" (90) to her actions, a necessary prerequisite for communication. She goes beyond cultural conditioning and, in committing the act of metaphor, implicitly commits herself to Tristero. Her willingness to sort impressions and clues and to eschew the easy acts of solipsism and mindless assimilation, the two forms of psychic death in *Lot 49*, are heroic. Most of the other characters—Mucho, Metzger, Driblette, Hilarius—succumb to one or both of these forms of escape. Oedipa, however, courageously confronts the possibility that her discoveries are hallucinations or paranoid designs, and continues her search. By coming to terms with who she is, she can go beyond self-enclosures and communicate.

In contrast to Inamorati Anonymous, in which isolates institute a system to insulate themselves against love, Oedipa's peregrinations through the underground lead her to a genuine act of love and communication. When she encounters the drunken sailor, she is "overcome all at once by a need to touch him" (126). Furthermore, she serves as guardian for his letter to his wife and, in doing so, becomes a messenger for the W.A.S.T.E. system, thereby entering the Tristero network in thought and in deed. From holding the sailor Oedipa discovers that he suffers from the DTs and, increasingly attuned to hieroglyphs, ponders the metaphor suggested by the initials. As a time differential in calculus dt means "a vanishing small instant in which change had to be confronted at last for what it was" (129). Unlike those who engage in avoidance behavior and who dull and secularize communication through relinquishing the self to the corporate conspiracy, Oedipa honestly confronts the responsibility she has as a constituent of an American culture that is losing its diversity. Inverarity's advice to her, "Keep it bouncing," turns out to be prophetic. To communicate, one must keep the flow of information cycling and learn to decipher the world's hieroglyphics while welcoming the fact that clues lead inevitably to further clues, that absolute answers are both illusory and stagnating.

In the course of her quest Oedipa assumes the role of a cultural Maxwell's Demon. This machine, which is in the dubious hands of John Nefastis, "connects the world of thermodynamics to the world of information flow . . . [and] makes the metaphor not only verbally graceful, but also objectively true" (106). Conceived by Scottish physicist James Clerk Maxwell in 1871, the Demon is a theoretical intelligence capable of distinguishing between slower and faster molecules, which it then can sort indefinitely into hot and cold, thereby creating a perpetual-motion machine and contravening the second law of thermodynamics. The Demon does what Oedipa must learn to do: consciously resist entropy by sense-making to keep the world bouncing. At this point in the novel, though, Oedipa is not yet a sensitive; her sense of herself is still too enmeshed in the inertia of the Tupperware-party mentality to play an active role in organizing the information she discovers. She still views herself as an

impotent victim lost in the world's indifferent and in-
comprehensible design, and avoids her responsibility
to participate in re-creating that design. The shape of
the novel is such that Oedipa grows from the high entropy and low individuality of the tower scene in
chapter 1 to the high individuality and large degree of
information of the conclusion.

Oedipa's instinctive reaction to comfort the
drunken sailor, like her decision to aid him in his act of
communication and her resolution to attend the crying of lot 49, is an act of faith akin to love. It requires
that she get outside herself, risk removing her protective insulation, and make herself vulnerable in order
to communicate. Her quest permits her to forge connections between worlds as well as to keep her own
life bouncing. In contrast to the subjective isolation of
a Driblette or a Hilarius or the cultural corrosion of
San Narciso, Oedipa tries to make sense of her world
and, in doing so, restores meaning to her sense of self.
At the end of the novel she once again confronts the
void. She decides that there are four alternative solu-
tions to the clues she has perceived, and she conceives
of them as binary pairs. Either (1) there is a vast underground network of exiles within the system or (2)
she is hallucinating it. Or (3) Tristero is an elaborate
plot, a hoax planned by Inverarity and directed at Oedipa. Indeed, the possibility exists that all of Oedipa's
informants may be Inverarity's agents, for he owns ev-

erything—Yoyodyne, Fangoso Lagoons, Zapf's Used Books, the Tank Theatre, the college at which Emory Bortz teaches. Or (4) Oedipa is as insane as Hilarius in her paranoid delusions. The impossibility of resolving these choices would have driven the earlier Oedipa into her tower, but this character has educated herself to commit the act of metaphor that leaps beyond mutually exclusive polarities. That all of these possibilities exist contributes more diversity, more information to the system. In a sense, any resolution becomes a form of death, an end to the quest that revivifies life and culture. Like all of Pynchon's major characters Oedipa must walk the fine line between establishing connections to organize and make sense of experience and allowing these connections to become rigid systems that interpret new information in a static fashion, yielding entropic stagnation.

Paranoia, or the imposition of design on random forces, can therefore be creative or destructive, depending on the individual's willingness to view these designs as heuristic aids to understanding. This willingness to view resolution not as an end in itself but as part of the process of sense-making renders expectations meaningless and the fear of loss delusory. Oedipa's decision to witness the crying of lot 49 is an affirmative act of faith undertaken "with the courage you find you have when there is nothing more to lose" (182).

THE CRYING OF LOT 49

Closing the text, an allusion to the miracle of Pentecost underscores the reader's sense that the Tristero experience has restored mystery to Oedipa's life, and potentially may so restore the culture at large. Pentecost occurs on the seventh Sunday (forty-nine days) after Easter, and the religious imagery that concludes *Lot 49* links the revelation of the Tristero agent's identity with an infusion of the sacred into the profane world of the auction. Like Oedipus, Oedipa has discovered how deeply implicated she is in what she finds. For Oedipus, knowledge of identity yields tragedy. For Oedipa, it offers a proliferation of metaphors that revivify her.

The fact that no revelation concludes the book, that it exists only in potential, fits the thematic design. An absolute answer would end the flow of information, replacing the ambiguity that is indigenous to postmodern realism with a certainty which would maximize entropy. All the modes of representation introduced in *Lot 49*—religion, history, art, language, thermodynamics, information theory—are subjected to the same uncertainty. The binary oppositions suggested at the conclusion—that Tristero is everything or nothing, that there is transcendence or only solipsism, that communication may occur or that there is merely a babble of signs—keep the reader bouncing. As with Oedipa, the act of interpretation becomes the act of metaphor, and, by causing the reader to commit

UNDERSTANDING THOMAS PYNCHON

that act, Pynchon imbues language with magic and communication with meaning.

Notes

1. Alfred MacAdam suggests that Jorge Luis Borges's story "The Approach to Al-Mu'tasim" provides the model for *The Crying of Lot 49* ("Pynchon as Satirist: To Write, to Mean," *Yale Review* 67 [1975]: 560).

2. Thomas Pynchon, *The Crying of Lot 49* (Philadelphia: Lippincott, 1966) 9. Further references will be noted parenthetically.

3. The seminal article for this discussion is Anne Mangel, "Maxwell's Demon, Entropy, Information: *The Crying of Lot 49*," *TriQuarterly* 20 (1971): 194–208.

4. C. G. Jung, "The Tibetan Book of the Dead: Psychological Commentary," *The Tibetan Book of the Dead*, ed. W. Y. Evans-Wentz (New York: Oxford University Press, 1960) xxxv.

CHAPTER FIVE

Gravity's Rainbow: Personal Density and the Arc of Preterition

"Mark, Reader, my cry! Bend thy thoughts on the Sky"

With its opening words, "A screaming comes across the sky," *Gravity's Rainbow* appeared in 1973 like a scorching prophecy, a literary Halley's Comet to be treated with fascination and fear. "It has happened before," when *Moby-Dick* and *Ulysses* took the pulse of their respective cultures and unraveled their disturbing and mystifying findings, "but there is nothing to compare it to now." For Pynchon, "it's all theatre, . . . not a disentanglement from, but a progressive *knotting into*."[1]

With its cast of some four hundred characters and its international scope *Gravity's Rainbow* attains epic proportions. Its theatrical frame comments on the violation of traditional novelistic design that is itself a commentary on the dangers inherent in system-building. The lack of decorum and the protean points of view become both entanglements for the reader and a means for self-discovery. Rational deduction, in its quest to attain distance in order to pronounce judgment, is shown to be reductive and destructive. While the novel is diffuse, baffling, and profoundly disturbing, these are not due to fallacies of composition but to calculated aims. Rather than attempting to justify the ways of God to men,[2] Pynchon's epic steps outside of received cultural assumptions in exposing justification to be no cause, but only an effect of potentially devastating proportions.

Gravity's Rainbow is arguably the most important novel to emerge during the postmodern period, and contains the self-consciousness that characterizes much of the fiction produced during this time. Although Pynchon's narrator is an omniscient reporter of the thoughts and deeds of his characters, the tone of the novel lacks consistency, abruptly shifting from gorgeous lyrical passages to mockery. Discontinuous events are run into one another, and the reader leaps across space and time with few transitions. The narrator will occasionally disengage himself from the narrative and address the reader, reminding him of the fictional construct with which he is dealing. In an otherwise sympathetic essay David Leverenz terms the book "an act of calculated hostility against my own need to find out what it is about."[3] It would be easy to

GRAVITY'S RAINBOW

assign this seeming lack of coherence to poor writing, as the Pulitzer Advisory Board and several critics have done,[4] or to attribute it to the report that Pynchon wrote most of *Gravity's Rainbow* while stoned.[5] Indeed, the original title for the novel was *Mindless Pleasures.* However, Pynchon's labyrinthine plot and elusive center respond to the sense of relativity that informs contemporary philosophy. All plots are fictions, imaginative constructs to order a world that tends toward disorder. As seen in *V.* and *The Crying of Lot 49*, metaphors in Pynchon's works are lies that serve as vehicles for truth.

Pynchon sets *Gravity's Rainbow* during the last nine months of World War II and the immediate postwar period in order to examine the gestation and birth of postmodern culture. Both structure and style illuminate theme, for the culture is in disarray, suffering paroxysms of self-annihilation. For all the sexual interactions that occur within its pages the novel is essentially loveless. The humor that permeates it exists in constant juxtaposition to the gravity of the situations it informs, as suggested by the novel's title. The parabola of the rainbow becomes a parable of the arc of history. As things fall apart and the center ceases to hold, to quote W. B. Yeats's "The Second Coming," the Old Testament sign of God's covenant with man now traces the flight of the V-2 rocket and, by implication, the other technological rough beasts that are its insidious heirs as they fall toward man's self-inflicted apocalypse.

For Pynchon the theater that our culture has become is simultaneously spectacular and minimalist, an absurd tragicomedy where waiting for the appearance of some Godot is a quest for suicide. Drawing from Norman O. Brown's Freudian suggestion in *Life Against Death* that repression is the essence of man, Pynchon employs gravity as a metaphor for the repression that forms the cornerstone of our cultural heritage.[6] Whether he is cloaked in the garb of Calvinist determinism, Nazi supremacy, or the multinational business cartel, in Pynchon's miracle play Repression is the primary allegorical figure who dominates the stage, raging through multiple soliloquies while Death waits in the wings.

However, as seen in Pynchon's two previous novels, he offers a fragile infrastructure that presents the possibility of hope in a resurgence of humanism to battle the masochistic passivity that repression has ingrained. Roger Mexico serves as the primary spokesman for this alternative in *Gravity's Rainbow*. His views are foreshadowed in the introduction of the first character in the novel, Pirate Prentice. On the roof of Prentice's abode in the center of war-torn London he cultivates bananas in a soil of manure, dead leaves, and vomit. His bananas thrive, sometimes reaching lengths of a foot and a half, and Pirate has become famous for his Banana Breakfasts, orgiastic feasts featuring every possible culinary variation performed on this bizarre fruit. As the phallic death force of the V-2 rockets, the "bright angel of death" (760), rapes London, the phallic banana offers comic evidence for the generative capacities of earth:[7]

Now there grows among all the rooms . . . the fragile, musaceous odor of Breakfast: . . . taking over not so much through any brute pungency or volume as by the high intricacy to the weaving of its molecules, sharing the conjuror's secret by which—though it is not often Death is told so clearly to fuck off—the living genetic chains prove even labyrinthine enough to preserve some human face down ten or twenty generations . . . so the same assertion-through-structure allows this war morning's banana fragrance to meander, repossess, prevail. Is there any reason not to open every window, and let the kind scent blanket all Chelsea? As a spell, against falling objects (10).

The wealth of allusions and the intellectual and historical expansiveness of *Gravity's Rainbow* have caused Edward Mendelson, who of all critics has written most intelligently concerning Pynchon, to classify it as an encyclopedic narrative along with Dante's *Commedia*, Rabelais's *Gargantua and Pantagruel*, Cervantes' *Don Quixote*, Goethe's *Faust*, Melville's *Moby-Dick*, and Joyce's *Ulysses*.[8] Noble company in-

deed. According to Mendelson, like these other encyclopedic narratives *Gravity's Rainbow* begins its
history from a position outside the culture whose literary focus it becomes. The rejections of the novel by
the Pulitzer Advisory Board and by other members of
the literary establishment as an affront to good taste
recall the indignant self-righteousness that characterized the public reception of *Ulysses* five decades earlier.
The history of literature offers countless examples of
this process whereby the threat to the cultural establishment, if significant enough to resist the initial condemnation by that establishment, will gradually be
assimilated, thereby softening any cataclysm. Yet the
assimilation affects change as the threat ironically becomes part of the system it had threatened. With the
publication of *Ulysses* ideas of how to structure a
work of fiction could never be what they were. The
shock waves produced by *Gravity's Rainbow* indicate
that it potentially has a similar degree of influence.

In its implicit attacks on the intellectual parochialism fostered by the western empirical tradition *Ulysses* provides an antecedent to *Gravity's Rainbow*. Both
Joyce and Pynchon seek escape from the limitations
imposed by too narrow conceptions of symbol and reality, and both encompass a wide range of seemingly
incompatible extremes in their work. Joyce, a stylistic
chameleon, imitates and parodies every stylistic tradition while ultimately subscribing to none. Pynchon

GRAVITY'S RAINBOW

uses Laurence Sterne and Joyce as his models for parody, deflating all norms, offering multiplicity and randomness so that patterns may be discovered only in redundancy. Pynchon, however, goes beyond his predecessors in demonstrating that the inherited ways of classifying experience, not only in literature but in all systems of classification, are hindrances, contributing factors to the chaos of experience rather than aids to functioning within it. Joyce pushed parody to the point of literary self-parody to show how the available styles and forms of literature were insufficient constraints in which to ossify the flow of life. Pynchon extends this perception from literature to all systems, whether in science, pop-culture, politics, or history, to show that any attempt at recording life is a form of rigidification and repression.

Gravity's Rainbow employs numerous complex plots and subplots with a plethora of motifs, images, and symbols in "a progressive knotting into" that produces those thematic subjects that recur in the aforementioned great encyclopedic works of western literature: (1) the heroic quest for knowledge for self-growth and for the salvation of the quester's society; (2) the ambiguity of such knowledge in an uncertain world; (3) the meaning of freedom; (4) the paradox of mutability being the only stable concept in life; (5) the betrayals that occur between generations; (6) the consequences of repression; (7) the uses and misuses of language; (8) the dangers of solipsism; (9) the perversions generated by man's misuse of nature; (10) the connections between the natural and supernatural worlds; and (11) the lessons of history and the consequences of ignoring those lessons.

Where *Gravity's Rainbow* differs in its treatment of these themes is in its lack of resolution. Slothrop literally disintegrates as a presence in the novel; the fate of Blicero (whom we encountered as Weissmann in *V.*) is never revealed, Pökler's search for his wife and daughter yields no results, and Enzian and Tchitcherine don't recognize each other when they meet. No problems are solved, no slackening of the underlying conflicts that cause destruction occurs. There appears to be little difference between the conditions that exist in peacetime and those in war. Again, *Ulysses* is a signpost on this twentieth-century track, for the Blooms never resolve their marital problems in the time frame of the novel and, like Slothrop, Stephen Dedalus disappears from the novel, his destiny unknown. However, the meeting of Stephen and Bloom and the favorable shift toward Bloom that occurs in Molly's soliloquy offer the reader an implicit sense of completion and hope. Completion and hope are neither implicit nor explicit in *Gravity's Rainbow*.

The novel is divided into four parts that offer a linear structure through which the protagonist journeys on his quest for meaning. The protagonist of

GRAVITY'S RAINBOW

Gravity's Rainbow is Lt. Tyrone Slothrop, an American intelligence officer stationed in London during the German rocket blitz at the end of World War II. As Baby Tyrone in 1920 Slothrop had been sold by his father to finance his future education at Harvard into the behaviorist clutches of Harvard psychologist Dr. Laszlo Jamf. Slothrop became the unknowing victim of an experiment in the study of infantile sexuality which preconditioned him to have erections in the presence of Imipolex G, a polymer that will later serve in the construction of a particular V-2 rocket. Slothrop currently keeps a map of London on which he attaches colored stars to mark the sites of his numerous sexual conquests. When the corporate authorities who benefit from and control the war effort recognize that each of Slothrop's stars corresponds to the site of a subsequent V-2 hit, they decide that he might be utilized to locate a revolutionary group of black rocket troops that they wish to destroy. They fund Edward Pointsman to manipulate Slothrop so that he finds rocket number 00000, the Schwarzgerät which is uniquely equipped with Imipolex G. Pointsman, a devotee of Pavlovian conditioning, leads a research group at The White Visitation, home of PISCES (Psychological Intelligence Schemes for Expediting Surrender), which conducts experiments on psychological warfare. He is after a Nobel Prize and schemes to interpret Slothrop's connection with the rocket hits to conclusively prove "the stone determinacy of every-thing, of every soul" (86). What frustrates his behav-ioristic reliance on cause and effect is that Slothrop's erections occur *before* the rockets strike.

As part of his attempt to determine Slothrop's af-finity with the rocket, Pointsman arranges for him to undergo an experiment to test the white American's re-action to blacks. In a hilarious spoof of psychoanaly-sis Pynchon has Slothrop drift into a memory of the Roseland Ballroom in Roxbury, Massachusetts, where young Harvard men, Jack Kennedy among them, would go to hear swing music. In the men's room of the Roseland, Slothrop drops his harmonica down the toilet and, in leaning over to fetch it, is subjected to threats of sodomy by numerous black men, including Malcolm X (who actually worked at the Roseland). Pynchon then imposes a variation of the Orpheus myth by having Slothrop escape by following his harp down the toilet into an underground world. Swim-ming through the fecal matter of Boston, Slothrop dis-covers a refuge for America's downtrodden, the preterite (those who have been passed over) who have been associated with waste and therefore repressed into the deepest recesses of the unconscious by the Calvinist elect. The Calvinist providential plan be-comes equated with the arc of the rocket, fueled by a Pointsmanlike devotion to the reduction of reality to binary oppositions of right/wrong, good/evil. The

GRAVITY'S RAINBOW

consequent repression of the dark side of the personality which threatens the self-righteous elect yields an unnatural lack of balance in the cultural consciousness. This consciousness becomes epitomized by the rocket soaring across the heavens to destory the heathen masses, a giant metallic phallus to eradicate any primitive sexual threat, a weapon born from the repressed shadowy recesses of the chosen to wield against projections of their own forces of unreason. The annihilation of that which mitigates against a neat, ordered world becomes therefore a self-annihilation. Manichean motives dictate emotional hara-kiri. For his epigraph to part 2, Pynchon uses Merian C. Cooper's statement to Fay Wray: "You will have the tallest, darkest leading man in Hollywood." *Gravity's Rainbow* demonstrates that we create our King Kongs out of a perverse magnification and projection of the neglected dark side of our personalities, which our cultural Calvinism then commands us to destory with weapons produced by the forces of reason but shaped by that very darkness they obsessively seek to obliterate.

Slothrop's colonial ancestor, William Slothrop, once herded his pigs to slaughter in Boston. He watched them rush "into extinction like lemmings, possessed not by demons but by trust for men, which the men kept betraying" (555), and came to despise the civilization that justified their slaughter. His heretical tract, *On Preterition*, argued holiness for the preterite, "these 'second Sheep,' without whom there'd be no elect" (555). The narrator asks, "Could he have been the fork in the road America never took, the singular point she jumped the wrong way from?" He goes on to suggest that the war-ravaged Zone of postwar Germany offers a parallel possibility: "Maybe for a little while all the fences are down, one road as good as another, the whole space of the Zone cleared, depolarized, and somewhere inside the waste of it a single set of coordinates from which to proceed, without elect, without preterite, without even nationality to fuck it up." (556). Yet William Slothrop was expelled from Massachusetts Bay Colony, and other menaces to the power of the self-appointed elect throughout the western world are also ruthlessly squashed.

Pynchon twice refers to Max Weber's theory of the routinization of charisma (325, 464), and the German sociologist's theories inform the condemnation of Calvinism that pervades the novel. Weber believed that man combats his alienation through his rationality so that he can erect new systems of meaning. The designs that he creates, however, can be too narrowly restricted and so concerned with control that they promote oppression. These instances are manifested by the establishment of bureaucracies for the purposes of self-perpetuation and to dictate homogeneity. Weber viewed Calvinist America as an example of this rigidity and considered its capitalist economics as a logical and self-referential by-product of the need to extend and profit from control.[9] What Weber is describing, of course, is a sociological version of thermodynamic entropy—a closed system in decline.[10] He goes on to postulate that times of great vexation tend to produce charismatic figures who counter or slow the process of decline by offering irrational alternatives to the fixed system. Hitler and the mania that he prompted in Germany is one such example. However, Weber theorized that the dominant rational process will eventually assimilate charismatic elements and routinize them. Edward Mendelson points out that while *Gravity's Rainbow* is about this rationalization of charismatic authority, as an encyclopedic narrative it also enacts the same process by disrupting literary culture before being assimilated into it.[11]

Through its amassing of detail and characters *Gravity's Rainbow* offers a democratic response to Calvinist preterition and brings it into relief as the motivating force behind the twentieth-century death wish. The comic story of Byron the Bulb's heroic resistance against the lightbulb cartel suggests that the conspiracy extends even beyond the realm of the animate. John Dillinger and King Kong are presented as archetypal preterite figures. Dillinger is killed because he threatens the mercantile system that preserves the power of the elect. Kong also must be removed because of the revelatory mirror that his gigantic presence forces the elite to behold. As Slothrop's descent down the toilet indicates, the elect consistently attempt to flush away their fears. However, these fears then find refuge in the unconscious, where they are nourished, and occasionally reemerge, distorted and deadly.

Pointsman enlists Slothrop in the search for the Schwarzgerät and sends him to the Casino Hermann Goering, a French resort recently reclaimed by the Germans. Slothrop agrees to undertake the assignment because he seeks the connection between Imipolex G and his past, a connection about which Pointsman, who knows Jamf's work, is aware. In essence, then, Slothrop's quest is simultaneously a search for his own identity. Typical of Pynchon's undercutting, however, is the fact that this heroic quest is undertaken by a schlemihl who begins his tour of the Zone attired in an authentic Hawaiian shirt. The links between colonialism and tourism discussed in the chapter on *V.* implicate Slothrop as an extension of the very web from which he wishes to extricate himself. But he is an unwitting tool of the warmongering conglomerate of business cartels, scientists, and politicians whose power seems so omnipresent that they come to be collectively referred to as "Them." Later, in Cuxhaven, Slothrop discovers that his movements have been monitored, and escapes.

GRAVITY'S RAINBOW

Pynchon's recurrent theme of paranoia inhabits every convoluted niche of *Gravity's Rainbow*. There is no clear distinction between settings during and after the war because the potential for destruction remains consistent. In his journey through the Zone, Slothrop comes to recognize that everywhere seems the same: "Richard Halliburton, Lowell Thomas, Rover and Motor Boys, jaundiced stacks of *National Geographics* up in Hogan's room must've all lied to him, and there was no one then, not even a colonial ghost in the attic, to tell him different." (266). Events are controlled by Them. The cultural mindset is easily manipulated, for They dictate the messages that are transmitted by the media. The economic productivity that occurs during wartime may be stimulated by fanning the flames of nationalism and by duping the preterite into thinking that they control their own destinies. Slothrop too is watched and manipulated. Pointsman arranges for him to rescue one of his spies, Katje Borgesius, from the tentacles of an octopus, but Slothrop eventually escapes Pointsman's surveillance and wanders the unpredictable Zone assuming a multitude of identities.

Slothrop's wanderings cease to have any direct purpose. His quest loses its object and he becomes a protean figure as his adventures grow increasingly extraordinary. Geli Tripping, the witch, tells him, "Forget frontiers now. Forget subdivisions. There aren't any. . . . You'll learn. It's all been suspended. Vaslav calls it an 'interregnum.' You only have to flow along with it" (294). By learning to flow, Slothrop abandons paranoia as a means of organizing and dictating experience. Shifting from discrete identity to a series of masks, he loses his resemblance to "any sort of integral creature" (740).

It is not in a name, but in the act of naming that power may be found, Slothrop is told (366). As he dons costume after costume, he moves from schlemihl to mythic force. At a ten-century-old festival which commemorates Thor's thunder-pig, Plechazunga, driving off a Viking raid in a small Baltic town, Slothrop becomes the Pig-Hero of the pagan preterite and saves the village from Nazi intruders. Later, still adorned in his pig suit, Slothrop becomes the trickster-hero. Chased by MPs, he ends up in the baths where the odious Major Marvy exerts the racism that springs from his attempts to suppress his own darkness by having sex with a Spaniard. Marvy escapes from the raid by dressing in Slothrop's pig suit. However, he is made to suffer for his theft. Pointsman's men, who are on a mission to procure Slothrop's testicles in another project generated by Pointsman's mania for the empirical, mistake him for Slothrop, capture and castrate him. As the cartoon hero Rocketman ("Fickt nicht mit der Raketemensch!" he proclaims), Slothrop spawns an underground legend which is confirmed by his discovery of "Rocketman was here" graffiti. He also plays the role of the Fool in the Tarot deck, moving through the various stages of experience symbolized by the primary cards of the deck—the major arcana. Indeed, after his disappearance, there is rumored to be a last photograph of him on the only record album ever put out by The Fool, an English rock group. Others speculate "that fragments of Slothrop have grown into consistent personae of their own" (742).

In his disintegration as a integral character and finally, as a presence in the novel, Slothrop comes to embody (or disembody) Pynchon's recurrent interest in entropy as a metaphor. The acronym indicated by the first syllable of Slothrop's name indicates this—Sloth = second law of thermodynamics.[12] His eventual scattering coincides with the dropping of the bomb on Hiroshima, the news of which is offered to him without his comprehension through a

scrap of newspaper headline, with a wirephoto of a giant white cock, dangling in the sky straight downward out of a white pubic bush. The letters
MB DRO
ROSHI (693).

The introduction of such a powerful force of destruction in the world, a force created through rational design, ironically challenges faith in all systems of belief. Like the newspaper headline the flood of information can now only be accepted piecemeal as a series of temporary signs subject to immediate displacement. The V-2 becomes, mutatis mutandis, the nuclear bomb. Pynchon makes it clear that the immediate user is irrelevant, for national identity has become a delusion employed by the international military industrial complex to manipulate the preterite. "True war is a celebration of markets," the reader is told. The Calvinistic attempts to constrain primitive sexual urges within the bounds of rational systems have perverted Eros into Thanatos, the bomb as "giant white cock" in the sky.[13]

A microcosm of the conversion of Eros to Thanatos can be observed aboard the *Anubis* (the name of the jackal-headed Egyptian god who presides over the embalming of the dead), on which Slothrop leaves Berlin with Margherita Erdmann. The *Anubis* carries a collection of refugees from the war who, like Slothrop, are tourists without destination: "We'll all just keep moving, that's all. In the end it doesn't matter," Slothrop is told by one passenger (479). Margherita had starred in a pornographic movie, *Alpdrücken* (Nightmare), the torture scene of which so aroused the film crew that she was gang raped, became pregnant, and bore Bianca, who is also aboard the *Anubis*. Ironically, this is the very film that arouses Franz Pökler and causes him to return home to his wife, Leni, and take her in a fantasy of having sex with Margherita. She also becomes pregnant and gives birth to Ilse, who serves as Bianca's shadow double in the novel. Children of fantasy become themselves fantasies. Pökler is never sure that it is his daughter with whom he is annually reunited, yet he persists in the fantasy for it is all that gives meaning to his life. Bianca mimics Shirley Temple for the entertainment of the passengers aboard the *Anubis*. For refusing an encore, she is spanked with a steel ruler onstage by Margherita, an act that sends the audience into an orgy. Bianca's innocence is also revealed to be illusory when she seduces Slothrop after her beating. And malleable Slothrop also gives himself up to fantasy with daughter and mother. At one point we find him whipping Margherita on the same movie set on which *Alpdrücken* was filmed sixteen years earlier. Later, Margherita's husband, Thanatz (Thanatos), proposes a theory of a community of Sado-anarchism that would undercut guilt, thus robbing the system of its power:

Why will the Structure allow every other kind of sexual behavior but *that* one? Because submission and dominance are resources it needs for its very survival. They cannot be wasted in private sex; . . . It needs our lusts after dominance so that it can co-opt us into its own power game; . . . I tell you, if S and M could be established universally, at the family level, the State would wither away (737).

Slothrop also has a vision of a City of the Future, "full of extrapolated 1930s swoop-façaded and balconied skyscrapers, lean chrome caryatids with bobbed hairdos, classy airships of all descriptions drifting in the boom and hush of the city abysses, golden lovelies sunning in roof-gardens and turning to wave as you pass. It is the Raketen-Stadt" (674). Among this debased phantasm of "plastic herbage" and "soft-plastic offices" lies a bleak redundancy of inanimate totems and inert decadence. The design derives from the same Calvinist dichotomy that informs Slothrop's earlier vision of his New England past:

slender church steeples poised up and down all these autumn hillsides, . . . rose windows taking in Sunday light, elevating and washing the faces above the pulpits defining grace, swearing *this is how it does happen—yes the great bright hand reaching out of the cloud* (29).

Through rationality the sacred has been divided from the mundane. The self-appointed elect claim access to it and enslave the preterite with routine service, dangling the Protestant ethic before them to encourage their labors. The dichotomy serves to preserve their power and to hold the masses in check, acquiescing to the despondent ordinariness of their lives in the hope of future infusions of grace. As mythic hero Slothrop is assigned "to rescue the Radiant Hour, which has been abstracted from the day's 24 by colleagues of the Father, for sinister reasons of their own" (674). But Slothrop is no savior. The heroic quest in postmodernism has been converted into a personal quest, the social ramifications of which are generally insignificant. With no objective reality, salvation is transformed from an absolute to a relative perspective.

According to Mondaugen's Law,

"personal density . . . is directly proportional to temporal bandwidth. 'Temporal bandwidth' is the width of your present, your *now*. . . . The more you dwell in the past and in the future, the thicker your bandwidth, the more solid your persona. But the narrower your sense of Now, the more tenuous you are" (509).

As Slothrop wanders the Zone, his personal density contracts. Like Fausto Maijstral in *V.*, he begins to view himself as a series of past identities: "Past Slothrops, say averaging one a day, ten thousand of them, some more powerful than others had been going over every sundown to the furious host" (624). Eventually, abandoning the paranoia of connective plots and drifting in the Now, he fades. Yet his disappearance is accompanied by a concentration of natural and supernatural imagery that seems to endorse his amorphous consciousness as an alternative to the tradition of Pointsmanlike bifurcation.

First, Slothrop finds the harmonica that he had dropped down the toilet in the Roseland Ballroom. In playing it he comes "closer to being a spiritual medium than he's been yet" (622). The narrator tells us that he is an embodiment of Rilke's prophesy in the *Sonnets for Orpheus:*

> And though Earthliness forget you,
> To the stilled Earth say: I flow.
> To the rushing water speak: I am (622).

Slothrop's personal density is not visible in an unnatural world gone mad through overreliance on rationalism. His Orphic quest loses cause and effect. For him Eurydices have vanished as either inducements or restraints. He finds himself projected as graffiti on the wall, "Rocketman was here," and scratches another legend, a mandala image of the rocket as seen from below (a mandala is a diagram of counterbalanced and concentric geometric figures, usually circles enclosing squares, that represents the Hindu conception of the universe as a synthesis of dualities). Like the cross and the swastika it is another fourfold image, an emblem of a culture. Slothrop himself becomes such a mandala emblem, "a crossroad" (626), his mythic connotations returned to the Orphic underground of the formless Zone. As a crossroad from past to present he represents the Hermetic unification of what is above and what is below that has been rent asunder by the intellectual parochialism of western reason. As a possible crossroad from present to future his concluding vision of the rainbow entering into sexual union with the earth is an affirmation, an antithesis to the rocket's annihilating penetrations: "Slothrop sees a very thick rainbow here, a stout rainbow cock driven down out of pubic clouds into Earth, green wet valleyed Earth, and his chest fills and he stands crying, not a thing in his head, just feeling natural (626).

Opposed to Pointsman's unflinching faith in determinism is the statistician Roger Mexico, who deals with random probabilities and views the coincidence between Slothrop's erections and rocket strikes as a statistical oddity. His rainbow arc is the Poisson distribution, a bell-shaped curve:

But to the likes of employees such as Roger Mexico it is music, not without its majesty, this power series $Ne^{-m} \left(1 + m + \frac{m^2}{2!} + \frac{m^3}{3!} + \ldots + \frac{m^{n-1}}{(n-1)!} \right)$, terms numbered according to rocketfalls per square, the Poisson dispensation ruling not only these annihilations no man can run from, but also cavalry accidents, blood counts, radioactive decay, number of wars per year (140).

Mexico views purely binary thinking as a limitation and proposes that "the next great breakthrough may

UNDERSTANDING THOMAS PYNCHON

come when we have the courage to junk cause-and-effect entirely, and strike off at some other angle" (89).

Roger's caring and contemplation make him the spokesman for humanism in the novel. However, his voice is not sustained, and when it does appear, it is frequently characterized by mournful isolation. In the lyrical scene where Roger and Jessica Swanlake attend an Advent service, his vision of transsubstantiation consists of piles of toothpaste tubes being metamorphosed into war products. Like the narrative voice of *Gravity's Rainbow*, which sarcastically nudges the reader for his reliance on cause and effect (663), Mexico recognizes the essential indeterminacy of life and the consequent obsession with reason to compensate for insecurities regarding the uncontrollable and unpredictable. He parallels Pynchon in viewing reason as an arbitrary and artificial construct, a closed system which is superimposed on the open, random nature of reality. As such, instead of mitigating meaninglessness, it ultimately exacerbates the predicament. During the service, Mexico contemplates the meeting of the Christ child and God. He muses, "Is the baby smiling, or is it just gas? Which do you want it to be?" (131). Beliefs then are situational responses within the vast realm of uncertainty. While Pointsman "can only possess the zero and the one," Mexico can "survive anyplace in between" (55).

GRAVITY'S RAINBOW

Mexico feels that his relationship with Jessica miraculously links him to the Now and offers him the sustenance to survive the states between:

His life had been tied to the past. He'd seen himself a point on a moving wavefront, propagating through sterile history—a known past, a projectable future. But Jessica was the breaking of the wave. Suddenly there was a beach, the unpredictable . . . new life. Past and future stopped at the beach: that was how he'd set it out. But he wanted to believe it too, the same way he loved her, past all words—believe that no matter how bad the time, nothing was fixed, everything could be changed and she could always deny the dark sea at his back, love it away. And (selfishly) that from a somber youth, squarely founded on Death— along for Death's ride—he might, with her, find his way to life and to joy (126).

However, Jessica views Roger as little more than an eccentric adventure and opts for the safety of the upper-class Jeremy. For Mexico, "Jeremy *is* the War, he is every assertion the fucking War has ever made—that we are meant for work and government, for austerity: and these shall take priority over love, dreams, the spirit, the senses" (177). The War is a state of mind, a communicable cancer that Roger sees Jessica "catching." For Jessica, peacetime is a signal to reaffirm a

sense of stability, to return to the secure confines of social clubs and bourgeois mores. But to Roger, "it's another bit of propaganda. . . . There's *something* still
on, don't call it a 'war' if it makes you nervous, maybe
the death rate's gone down a point or two . . . but
Their enterprise goes on" (628). In *Gravity's Rainbow*
love becomes a momentary encounter, a collision of
fantasies that are unable to sustain their convergence.
Ultimately the characters, both heroes and villains,
are isolated, treading "the path you must create by
yourself, alone in the dark" (136).

Mexico's antagonism toward the conglomerate
that creates and motivates a culture predicated on
stringent patterns of reason born of fear leads him to
join the Counterforce, an anarchic collection of coun-
terinsurgents devoted to irrationality. Osbie Feel
screams, "We piss on Their rational arrangements"
(639), and Mexico, when he intrudes on a corporation
meeting, jumps on the conference table and urinates
on the wielders of power. Later, he and Pig Bodine infiltrate a formal dinner party of corporate executives
and unleash a stream of alliterative culinary gro-
tesques, including "snot soup," "pus pudding," "men-
strual marmalade," and "ringworm relish." The diners
leave with napkins over their mouths. Yet the Counterforce, like the They-system it rebels against, is
monolithic, the opposite end of a polarity. Toward the
end of the novel the reader finds it assimilated, its rep-

GRAVITY'S RAINBOW

resentatives qualifying assertions with bureaucratic latinisms: "We were never that concerned with Slothrop *qua* Slothrop" (738).

The relationship between Tchitcherine and his half-brother, Enzian, offers another example of the destruction wrought by the denial of the dark side of the self. Tchitcherine's father had had a lapse in his attention to his duties aboard a coal ship in 1904 and had gone ashore and impregnated a Herero girl, a momentary indiscretion with reverberating consequences. Shortly thereafter he is killed in a naval attack in Port Arthur. Tchitcherine seems made of technology, reminiscent of the Bad Priest in *V.:* "more metal than anything else. Steel teeth wink as he talks. Under his pompadour is a silver plate. Gold wirework threads in three-dimensional tattoo among the fine wreckage of cartilage and bone inside his right knee joint" (337). A white, civilized Russian who works with machinelike efficiency for Soviet intelligence, he becomes obsessed with finding and destroying the black, primitive Herero who represents the unreasonable and therefore intolerable part of his personality. His Manichean quest echoes throughout *Gravity's Rainbow*, perhaps most poignantly when Pirate Prentice taps the ancestral memory of Katje Borgesius, a descendant of Franz van der Groov. In the seventeenth century the Dutchman, van der Groov, exterminated the dodo bird population because the birds appeared too ugly to be part of

God's grand design. His Calvinist mission was one of murder to create order, a microcosm of the colonial impulse throughout the western hemisphere.

Joseph Slade identifies a primary subplot of *Gravity's Rainbow* as the colonial oppression through linguistics, and invokes Walter Ong's theory that the "desacralization of culture" began with the development of the alphabet.[14] Tchitcherine's promotion of the acceptance of the New Turkic Alphabet (complete with bureaucratic acronym—NTA) while stationed on the steppes of Central Asia presents one such example of this loss of the sacred. By depicting the imposition of a standardized alphabet to replace unwritten speech and gesture, Pynchon demonstrates the undermining of cultural heritage. The inimical power of colonialism lies in its capacity and desire to invade the viscera of a civilization, to bring "the State to live in the muscles of your tongue" (384). In snatching the lifeblood of language from its colonies, the State (the They-system) facilitates its control by destroying their aberrant variety. A flat one-dimensionality is thereby created; easy to manipulate, but entropic in its sameness.

Tchitcherine's quest to eradicate his half-brother is given a counterdimension by his mystical experience with the Kirghiz Light in the steppes of Central Asia. So rigid is his mental constitution that he is subject to extremes without ever achieving balance, hence

GRAVITY'S RAINBOW

his subsequent susceptibility to Geli Tripping's spells. His attempt to reach the Kirghiz Light acquires the religious connotations of a pursuit of a Holy Grail that will transform him utterly. However, Pynchon again frustrates resolution. Although Tchitcherine reaches the light, he is not reborn. His heart is not ready. While he turns again to tracking his alter ego, his unconscious yearnings for metamorphosis respond to Geli's magic which reveals the transformations of the earth. The charms of Geli, "the only one in the Zone who loves him completely" (719), can defuse Tchitcherine's crusade against darkness. In the reader's final encounter with Tchitcherine he and Geli lie blissfully together while Enzian and the Schwarzkommando pass by. The brothers never recognize each other. Tchitcherine hustles cigarettes and potatoes for the night from Enzian and returns to Geli. Indeed, the power of the irrational to counter the destructive plans of the rational mind informs the history within and behind *Gravity's Rainbow*. Hitler, who ironically is seldom mentioned in this novel set at the conclusion of World War II, dreamt that the V-2 would not fly and delayed funding for the scientists at Peenemünde for two years, a delay which may have cost Germany the war.[15]

Enzian serves as a Moses figure for the Hereros, and attempts to lead them in an exodus from the bondage of colonialism through the creation of a technological totem, the 00001 rocket.[16] As Blicero's lover in Southwest Africa, Enzian returned with him to Germany, where he was trained as a rocket specialist. In the present action of the novel he attempts to save his people by founding a black rocket corps, the Schwarzkommando, and through construction of a replica of Blicero's 00000 rocket to counter its destructive potential. His paradoxical nature is implicit in his name. *Enzian* is both the German for the mountain gentian immortalized in Rilke's poetry and the name of a twelve-foot-long surface-to-air missile that was rejected for the V-2.

The history of the Hereros "is one of lost messages" (322). Their mantra, "Mba-kayere," means "I am passed over" (362) and links them to the preterite of the west. Their suppression by the German occupation forces has alienated them from the natural processes that constitute their religion. One group, led by Josef Ombindi, call themselves the Empty Ones and are dedicated to racial suicide: "prophets of masturbating, specialists in abortion and sterilization, pitchmen for acts oral and anal, pedal and digital, sodomistical and zoophiliac" (318). Their life-denying proselytizing begins to make sense to the rest of the tribe who are "exiled in the Zone, Europeanized in language and thought, split off from the old tribal unity" (318).

In adopting technology as a religion, Enzian hopes "the people will find the Center again" (319). By

making the rocket holy, he hopes to lead his Erd-
schweinhöhlers (named for the Herero symbol of fer-
tility, the aardvark or earth pig) out of the wasteland
of colonial occupation and the death wish of the Empty
Ones. Enzian realizes that the repression of his people
is but one instance of the repression of all the preterite
of the earth to serve the vampiric needs of the power
elite. He understands that it is not politics that dictates
war:

The politics was all theatre, all just to keep the people
distracted . . . secretly, it was being dictated instead
by the needs of technology . . . by a conspiracy between human beings and techniques, by something
that needed the energy-burst of war, crying, "Money
be damned, the very life of [insert name of Nation] is
at stake," but meaning, most likely, *dawn is nearly
here, I need my night's blood, my funding, funding,
ahh more, more* (521).

Enzian's vision dovetails with Slothrop's graffiti,
for the rocket to him is a replica of the shape of the
Herero village, a mandala.[17] He perceives his Erd-
schweinhöhlers as akin to Kabbalists, "the scholar-
magicians of the Zone" (520). Their holy Text is the
Rocket. The magical rejuvenative powers of the 00001,
derived from the unified mandalic vision of a cult
which marries the supernatural to the natural, would
counter the flight of the 00000, created by a sterile system of reason as a godless weapon to use against the

earth. When he learns from Thanatz about the firing of the Schwarzgerät with Gottfried aboard, a culminating event of the novel which the reader is not permitted to witness, he prepares for the firing of the 00001. Of course, Pynchon never allows his reader to witness this firing either, and the implication that Enzian will be a solitary passenger to counter the flight of Gottfried is also not confirmed.

Franz Pökler's story is one of the most touching in the novel. It begins in postwar 1945 with Pökler waiting in the ravaged Zwölfkinder amusement park for the seventh annual visit of his daughter, Ilse. True to the film motif that pervades Pökler's story and *Gravity's Rainbow* as a whole, the section proceeds as a montage of flashes between past and present. Pökler, a rocket engineer and "cause-and-effect man" (159), is left by Leni, whose less rational pursuits he continually rejects. The object of her new affection, Peter Sachsa, is a psychic medium and communist who is subsequently killed in a street demonstration. Leni and Ilse are then interned in a "re-education" camp. While Leni goes on in later years to become the whore Solange in Berlin, Pökler is controlled by the evil Blicero, who uses Ilse as a hostage. Blicero realizes that he will eventually need a plastics specialist to modify the 00000 for its future passenger and rewards Pökler for his work each August by allowing him to meet Ilse at the Zwölfkinder. The irony associated with these visits is that

Ilse, who was conceived through film-inspired lust, herself appears to Pökler as a series of movie frames:

A daughter a year, each one about a year older, each time taking up nearly from scratch. The only continuity has been her name, and Zwölfkinder, and Pökler's love—love something like the persistence of vision, for They have used it to create for him the moving image of a daughter, flashing him only these summertime frames of her, leaving to him to build the illusion of a single child (422).

Her identity is ultimately uncertain. She may indeed be a series of substitutes, yet he must content himself with the possible illusion that it is his daughter, for it is all he has to live for. A narrative gap of about 150 pages between Pökler's appearances underscores his loneliness. Near the end of this section neither Ilse nor her present incarnation has arrived, and Pökler's pig instead brings him Slothrop. Pynchon then gives us a flashback of Pökler wandering around the Dora concentration camp searching for his wife and daughter. He finds only a dying woman to whom he gives his wedding ring: "if she lived, the ring would be good for a few meals, or a blanket, or a night indoors, or a ride home" (433). Pynchon, the consummate jokester and parodist, leaves the reader heartbroken with this realistic portrayal.

That Pökler is a "fanatical movie hound" (577), that Ilse and Bianca are conceived from and become illusions, that Pökler and Leni are portrayed viewing Fritz Lang's *The Woman in the Moon*, that Tchitcherine's intelligence headquarters turns out to be a movie set, that the reader is told of Mitchell Prettyplace's definitive eighteen-volume study of *King Kong* certainly fit in a novel that states "it's all theatre" on its opening page and that concludes in a Los Angeles theater awaiting the end of the world. According to David Cowart, *Gravity's Rainbow* contains allusions to twenty-five movies, nine directors, and forty-eight actors and actresses.[18] The chapters within the novel are separated by graphics that look like film sprocket holes. The epigraph of part 3 as the reader enters the Zone is from *The Wizard of Oz* and contains an implicit nod to "Somewhere over the Rainbow." Yet these are not a collection of random references, for Pynchon uses film as a metaphor for how we choose (and perhaps are chosen) to live our lives.

Pynchon links film and the calculus used to invent the rocket as "pornographies of flight" (567): "There has been this strange connection between the German mind and the rapid flashing of successive stills to counterfeit movement, for at least two centuries—since Leibniz, in the process of inventing calculus, used the same approach to break up the trajectories of cannonballs through the air" (407). In

GRAVITY'S RAINBOW

undercutting Zeno's proof of the impossibility of the continuity of motion. Leibniz unknowingly performed a function that would unleash a concatenation of events, resulting in the nuclear age. The thought that there is a conspiracy of otherworldly dark forces to steer these events to some sinister conclusion becomes the most horrifying form of paranoia present in the book. The narrator tells us, "It was impossible not to think of the Rocket without thinking of *Shicksal*, of growing toward a shape predestined and perhaps a little otherworldly" (416). This malevolent design is also seen in Kekulé's dream in 1865 that revealed to him the molecular structure of benzene. It is "the meanness, the cynicism with which this dream is to be used" (412) that Pynchon laments, for it gives rise to the field of aromatic chemistry and then to the German dye industry that becomes the conglomerate IG Farben, currently funding Pointsman and violating the unifying cycle inherent in the archetypal nature of the dream. The conspiracies of darkness proliferate. The symbol for the double-integrating circuit in the guidance system of the rocket, a sign that is equated with the Nazi SS emblem, becomes the design of Albert Speer's weapons factory. Is the meanness and cynicism directed from above? Pynchon states that "it was nice of Jung to give us the idea of an ancestral pool in which everybody shares the same dream material. But how is it we are each visited as individuals, each by exactly and only what he needs? Doesn't that imply a switching-path of some kind? a bureaucracy?" (410). Even IG Farben attempts communion with the otherworld. In a séance in Berlin, Peter Sachsa calls up the spirit of Walter Rathenau, whose social ideas helped bring about the cartelized state. However, Rathenau's experience with the spirit world has expanded his vision beyond the circumscribed linear view of the self-serving businessmen to whom he speaks. His talk of process and his statement that "cause and effect is secular history, and secular history is a diversionary tactic" (167) meet with disdain and a lack of comprehension. As the initial epigraph in the novel from Wernher von Braun demonstrates, Pynchon embraces the idea of transformation, of "the continuity of our spiritual existence after death." *Gravity's Rainbow,* however, suggests bureaucracies among the dead as well as the living, a spiritual cartel that affects "death-by-government—a process by which living souls unwillingly become the demons known to the main sequence of Western magic as the Qlippoth, Shells of the Dead" (176). This paranoiac vision therefore proffers a presence lurking behind the downward spiral of the twentieth century.

In its illusion of continuity film is also used to comment on the duplicity of rational analysis. The book increasingly becomes a frustration to the reader's attempts to impose the rational crutch of determinacy on it. Characters shift roles, spatial and temporal continuity lapses, and tone metamorphoses. In the final fifth of the novel various ends of subplots are pasted together and slapstick scenes are introduced. Though connections are loose, everything seems somehow connected. However, once a system of analysis is applied, the rest of the fabric unravels around it. Gerhardt von Goll both makes films and deals drugs, two ways of altering the fixed consciousness of rational thinking. In his film, *New Dope* the direction of the images is reversed, a violation of cause and effect akin to that of the V-2 rocket, which is heard approaching *after* it explodes, like "a few feet of film run backwards" (48). At its conclusion the novel itself is equated to a film and reveals its readers to be its viewers. With the film broken or the projector bulb burnt out, the reader loses the comfort of the illusion and is forced out of his or her passive absorption of images to confront the eerie suspension of motion, the freeze frame that is the pale specter of his or her life. As in the theaters of old, everybody is invited to join in song, a linking together of the preterite against the splintering force of the rocket that bears down on them.

The obsession with the scatological in the pages of *Gravity's Rainbow* becomes a comment on "shit, money, and the Word, the three American truths" (28). The latter two function to suppress correlations with the former. The reader first encounters Points-man with his foot stuck in a toilet, observes Slothrop's descent down the toilet, is told of the floating German Toiletship, and experiences a linguistic discourse on the meaning of "Shit and Shinola." The Word divides the sacred from the profane, and the Calvinist heritage grapples with ways to widen the gap in order to repress fears of blackness and death. Yet, as Pynchon continually demonstrates, obsessive attempts to suppress the Other translate into projections of the Self. Katje Borgesius's Domina Noctura scene with Brigadier General Pudding is the novel's most shocking, and therefore most memorable, depiction of the masochistic self-hatred fostered by this Calvinist dichotomy.

Pudding lives in a state of self-torment for having sacrificed 70 percent of the soldiers under his command in the Battle of Ypres in World War I. In his retirement he attempts to write a book entitled *Things That Can Happen in European Politics*, a task that by its nature guarantees incompletion. At the beginning of World War II, Pudding volunteers and is assigned to The White Visitation. His dissatisfaction with this appointment is manifested in his daydreams during the rambling staff meetings, daydreams replete with guilty memories of the muddy and death-strewn battlefields of Flanders, filled with the terrible smell of corpses and human excrement. During the night he literally tastes his memories and indulges his resultant masochism by visiting his Mistress of the Night. Under the omnipresent direction of Pointsman, Katje dresses in the garb of a pornographic disciplinarian to receive Pudding, naked "except for a long sable cape and black boots . . . Her only jewelry is a silver ring with an artificial ruby not cut to facets but still in the original boule, an arrogant gout of blood, extended now, waiting his kiss" (233). After kissing Katje's boots, Pudding is whipped and drinks her urine. Then, aided by Pointsman's laxatives, Katje offers her excrement for him to eat while kneeling. It is a scene of sickening and frightening intensity that brings the consequences of guilt and obsession into grim relief.[19] Pudding's perversity testifies to his death wish, which is fulfilled in June, 1945, when he dies "of a massive *E. coli* infection" (533) induced by his ritualistic coprophagia. His Aryan consciousness exacerbates his need to be mustered with the ranks of the elect. Having failed in his duty on the battlefield and fallen into the realm of the profane, Pudding punishes himself by swallowing his memories in the form of the offal which he also considers a self-definition.

The conspiracy of darkness envelops Katje, converting her to "corruption and ashes" (94) as Blicero's Gretel, Pudding's Domina Noctura, and Pointsman's spy. With the exception of Geli Tripping, the fertile healing power of the Feminine is subverted throughout *Gravity's Rainbow* by phallic extirpations. Geli's dalliance with the supernatural equips her with an alternative perspective that contains a healthy organicism and an impulse to merge rather than divide. Love has become a spell, an arcane mystery divorced from everyday human activity which she employs to soothe the hate-ridden obsessions of Tchitcherine. Despite her activities in the Counterforce, the reader never knows whether Katje frees herself from the pernicious web that is analytically woven by Them. Although she escapes Blicero's perversions, Pirate Prentice's rescue of her seems engineered by Pointsman's forces. Prentice receives a message from Katje inside a cylinder that remains from the novel's first rocket strike. The message is written in invisible ink that only becomes visible in conjunction with his semen, and his arousal has been carefully prepared for by the enclosure of an erotic drawing of someone who resembles his lost love, Scorpia Mossmoon. Prentice asks himself, "Could there be, somewhere, a dossier, could They (They?) somehow have managed to monitor everything he saw and read since puberty?" (72). The evidence offered by the novel lends credence to this paranoid supposition. Katje's rescue, therefore, is hardly that at all. It is simply an exchange of one form of manipulation for another. At The White Visitation she participates in Pudding's self-humiliation and is secretly filmed by Teddy Bloat to program the octopus

GRAVITY'S RAINBOW

Grigori for attack, after which she seduces Slothrop as Pointsman's spy. Katje's beauty and sensitivity are converted from natural attributes that elicit joy and sharing to inimical tools for pain and control. Male dominance, characterized by overreliance on rationality as a consequence of rejection of the dark side, aggressively inserts itself into the creative and nourishing realm of the Feminine and prostitutes that realm to proliferate the war. Pynchon permits his reader only glimpses into an occasional hiatus from the brutal rape of culture, but they are magical glimpses characterized by caring and acceptance.

Gravity's Rainbow tells the story of the degeneration of the western world, a degeneration that culminates in the Nazi consciousness which erases national and historical boundaries to infect the world. Weissmann (white man) is an archetypal messenger of this death wish, a purveyor of colonial oppression and a perverter of love. He adopts Blicero as his SS code name because of its relation to "Blicker," the nickname the early Germans gave to Death (322). In Southwest Africa, infatuated with the *Duino Elegies*, he interprets Rilke's City of Pain through the Nazi vision that "every true god must be both organizer and destroyer" (99), and participates in the calculated destruction of Herero culture. When he returns to Germany with his black lover, Enzian, he begins his quest for immortality through the building of the Schwarzgerät. Blicero seeks to overcome the transitory, "to leave this cycle of infection and death" (724) and, as a master of transformation, to become like Rilke's angels that exist in the juncture between life and death. His ability to shift between extremes is demonstrated in his choice of lovers. Gottfried (God's peace), a gold-haired, blue-eyed Aryan, replaces Enzian the Herero and, with Katje as Gretel, plays Hansel to Blicero's abusive witch. As a boy-innocent Gottfried fulfills the romantic urge toward sublime death that Blicero gleans from Rilke and that furthermore links him with Slothrop, another sacrificial victim to the domain of Imipolex G. Blicero carefully engineers the symbolism within the polymer-lined chamber which shrouds Gottfried as he launches him at Lüneburg Heath toward his transformation:

Deathlace is the boy's bridal costume. . . . He is gagged with a white kid glove. . . . The glove is the female equivalent of the Hand of Glory, which second-story men use to light their way into your home: a candle in a dead man's hand, erect as all your tissue will grow at the first delicious tongue-flick of your mistress Death. The glove is the cavity into which the Hand fits, as the 00000 is the womb into which Gottfried returns (750).

While Slothrop is unable to comprehend the news of Hiroshima, Blicero understands it as the act that catapults America beyond innocence into Thanatos: "America *was* the edge of the World" (722). As the New World it "was a gift from the invisible powers, a way of returning" for Europeans to an Edenic state, cleansed of their colonial sins. But instead, "Europe came and established its order of Analysis and Death," a structure which America adopted and extended over the world. In Blicero's vision the edge, "our new Deathkingdom" (723), will be the moon. The pioneering spirit and impulse to start fresh in a new land will again be corrupted by the demands of cartelized analysis. The mania of rationalism for categories and hierarchies will once again establish a system of elect and preterite, predicated upon an urge toward exclusion rather than inclusion. The forces of oppression and death, then, become inevitable consequences of rigid adherence to fixed systems, an entropy of consciousness.

Blicero's Tarot card is the World, for the dream of death is everywhere. Thanatz considers him "the Zone's worst specter. He is malignant, he pervades the lengthening summer nights. Like a cankered root he is changing, growing toward winter, growing whiter, toward the idleness and the famine" (666). Imaginative and brilliant, Blicero is Pynchon's most insidious villain. For him, pleasure is the product of pain, and the sublime may be discovered only in the blank regions of death. His vision of immortality fosters decay. As a

UNDERSTANDING THOMAS PYNCHON

romantic for whom love is measured only in terms of control, he generates a seductive and sinister appeal. He is the archetypal Nazi within the collective unconscious of the preterite, promising quick and superficial panaceas to a group whose yearning for self-esteem contributes to their gullibility. And he is the spirit of the elect, a solipsistic and cynical confidence man bent entirely on self-glory and the enslavement of the Other. For Pynchon, Blicero is the face behind the mask of civilization that our culture wears. His unveiling is a warning that, as the descending rocket indicates, comes too late.

In response to Pig Bodine's statement that "*everything* is some kind of plot," Solange née Leni adds, "But, the arrows are pointing all different ways" (603). The text of the novel coalesces around its refusal to coalesce. The implication inherent in this is that interpretation as a stay against confusion fosters entropic and delusory patterns in its effort to harness the flux of life. The Counterforce's "Book of Memorabilia" which replaces Slothrop is one example of *Gravity's Rainbow's* commentary on its own powers of seduction. The book (Pavlov's second series of "Lectures on Conditioned Reflexes"[20]), a sacred text to its seven owners, becomes an emblem for the conversion of variety and mystery into the limited empirical categories that constitute Pointsman's conception of the universe. The Schwarzkommando also begin to view their rocket as a text. However, like the novel that it represents in microcosm, "its symmetries, its latencies, the *cuteness* of it enchanted and seduced us while the real Text persisted, somewhere else, in its darkness, our darkness" (520). It is toward this darkness that Pynchon steers us by jamming the signals to which our sense-making apparatus is customarily attuned.

Joseph Slade's theory that the narrator of *Gravity's Rainbow* is a Vietnam veteran "strung out on mysticism and dope,"[21] which is based on the passage "Between two station-marks, yellow crayon through the years of grease and passage, 1966 and 1971, I tasted my first blood" (739), is inaccurate but suggestive. The passage occurs when Pynchon injects himself into the mind of a spokesman for the Counterforce during an interview. He muses, "I am betraying them all . . . the worst of it is that I know what your editors want, *exactly* what they want," and then fantasizes about hunting down editors as an initiation into the Underground. Pynchon is fully aware of his position as a charismatic guerrilla writer, bent on the overthrow of the comfortable bourgeois reader to force him to reexamine his world. His concluding thought in this reflective soliloquy, "Do you want to put this part in?" is a typical comment on a comment, a self-deprecating nod to paranoia that is one characteristic of the narrative voice. Like his chiding the reader for relying on cause and effect (663) or his sudden telescoping into narrative distance to tell the reader to check out Ishmael Reed on Masonic mysteries (588), it is a reminder that the work is a fiction and thereby deconstructs the illusion that Pynchon has worked so hard to establish. Elsewhere the reader witnesses cacophony, a shifting narrative voice that adapts itself to the characters with whom it comes into proximity, a version of what Hugh Kenner has termed in his discussion of Joyce the "Uncle Charles Principle."[22] Slade's theory regarding the Vietnam veteran as narrator fails to note that the passage from which the theory is derived is self-referential in that the years 1966–1971 are those during which *Gravity's Rainbow* was composed. It is helpful, however, in that it offers an analogue for the experience of the reader as manipulated by Pynchon's guerrilla tactics.

The novel works on the reader's sensibilities to produce something akin to a mind in shock, reeling obsessively into a collapse of comprehension, then drifting off into a lyrical dream before discovering it to be a nightmare. Cultural preconceptions are shattered in an intellectual synesthesia. Multiple plots and points of view, jumps over space and through time, destroy familiar patterns of orientation so that the reader cannot get outside the novel, yet is consistently attempting entrances into it. He or she imbibes the malevolent war mentality through the perspective of the Zone. The details of war implant themselves in memory, yet the mind in the Zone is so glazed by their intensity that it responds defensively against the rational polarities that spawned the horror and functions by association rather than logic. Madness disguised as reason reveals itself as madness when its scaffolding, which the reader has helped to construct in the name of social or literary acceptability and on which he or she also habitually perches, is suddenly dynamited. It is then that the Kurtzlike vision of Blicero may be seen not as anomalous but as knit into the basic patterns of belief from which our cultural assumptions proceed.

The archetype of this vision is the rocket which plummets closer and closer to the theater that the reader has fabricated to ward off his or her responsibility for its existence. When the film stops and the illusion of the fiction is dispelled, *Gravity's Rainbow* offers the reader the choice between imminent destruction and the necessity of creating new mandalas. The preterite are asked to merge disparities through joining in song. The hymn they are invited to sing speaks of a healing synthesis, a resurrection of the unity of heaven and earth. Pynchon places his readers in the theater and leaves them suspended, with mouths open and eyes turned upward.

Notes

1. Thomas Pynchon, *Gravity's Rainbow* (New York: Viking, 1973) 3. Further references will be noted parenthetically.

2. Molly Hite calls *Gravity's Rainbow* "a modernist theodicy," a twentieth-century response to *Paradise Lost* (*Ideas of Order in the Novels of Thomas Pynchon* [Columbus: Ohio State University Press, 1983] 114).

3. David Leverenz, "On Trying to Read *Gravity's Rainbow*," *Mindful Pleasures*, ed. George Levine and David Leverenz (Boston: Little, Brown, 1976) 230.

4. Douglas Fowler argues that the book can be better understood when approached as a long poem (*A Reader's Guide to Gravity's Rainbow* [Ann Arbor: Ardis, 1980]).

5. Jules Siegel, "Who Is Thomas Pynchon . . . and Why Did He Take Off with My Wife," *Playboy* Mar. 1977: 172.

6. See Lawrence C. Wolfley, "Repression's Rainbow: The Presence of Norman O. Brown in Pynchon's Big Novel," *PLMA* 92 (1978): 873–89.

7. Tony Tanner also points this out in *Thomas Pynchon* (New York: Methuen, 1982) 89.

8. Edward Mendelson, "Gravity's Encyclopedia," ed. Levine and Leverenz 161–95.

9. Max Weber, *The Theory of Social and Economic Organization*, trans. A. M. Henderson and Talcott Parsons (New York: Oxford University Press, 1947) 358–92.

10. Joseph W. Slade shows this relationship in *Thomas Pynchon* (New York: Warner, 1974) 180.

11. Mendelson 177.

12. Daniel Simberloff points this out in "Entropy, Information and Life: Biophysics in the Novels of Thomas Pynchon," *Perspectives in Biology and Medicine* 21 (1978): 617.

13. See Herbert Marcuse, *Eros and Civilization* (Boston; Beacon Press, 1955) and Joseph W. Slade's discussion of its application to *Gravity's Rainbow* in "Religion, Psychology, Sex, and Love in *Gravity's Rainbow*," *Approaches to Gravity's Rainbow*, ed. Charles Clerc (Columbus: Ohio State University Press, 1983): 189–92.

14. Slade, "Religion, Psychology, Sex" 156. On p. 152 Slade refers to Walter J. Ong, *The Presence of the Word: Some Prolegomena to Cultural and Religious History* (New York: Simon and Schuster, 1967) 162.

15. Hite 107 points this out.

16. Fowler, 68–69 argues for the link between Enzian and Moses.

17. Thomas H. Schaub points out that Pynchon was drawing from H. G. Luttig's *The Religious System and Social Organization of the Herero* (Utrecht, 1933) in his depiction of Herero culture and religion (*Pynchon: The Voice of Ambiguity* [Urbana: University of Illinois Press, 1981] 85–86.

18. David Cowart, *Thomas Pynchon: The Art of Allusion* (Carbondale: Southern Illinois University Press, 1980) 33. Cowart's chapter on *Gravity's Rainbow* treats the novel directly through the metaphor of film. Clerc has an excellent essay, "Film in *Gravity's Rainbow*," in *Approaches to Gravity's Rainbow* 103–151. John O. Stark also offers a worthwhile discussion of the function of film in the novel (*Pynchon's Fiction: Thomas Pynchon and the Literature of Information* [Athens: Ohio University Press 1980] 132–45).

19. Paul Fussell offers an excellent commentary on this scene in *The Great War and Modern Memory* (New York: Oxford University Press, 1975) 329–33.

20. Mendelson 182 makes this identification and discusses its significance.

21. Slade, "Religion, Psychology, Sex" 160.

22. Hite 143 astutely makes this connection. Hugh Kenner discusses the Uncle Charles Principle in *Joyce's Voices* (Berkeley: University of California Press, 1978) 18.

BIBLIOGRAPHY

Works by Thomas Pynchon

Books

V. Philadelphia: Lippincott, 1963; London: Cape, 1963.

The Crying of Lot 49. Philadelphia: Lippincott, 1966; London: Cape, 1967.

Gravity's Rainbow. New York: Viking, 1973; London: Cape, 1973.

Mortality and Mercy in Vienna. London: Aloes Books, 1976.

Low-Lands. London: Aloes Books, 1978.

Slow Learner. Boston: Little, Brown, 1984.

Selected Periodical Appearances

"Mortality and Mercy in Vienna." *Epoch* 9 (Spring 1959): 195–213.

"The Small Rain." *Cornell Writer* Mar. 1959: 14–32.

"Low-Lands." *New World Writing* 16 (1960): 85–108.

"Entropy." *Kenyon Review* 22 (1960): 277–92.

"Togetherness." *Aerospace Safety* (Dec. 1960): 6–8.

"Under the Rose." *Noble Savage* 3 (1961): 223–51.

"The Secret Integration." *Saturday Evening Post* 19 Dec. 1964: 36–37, 39, 42–44, 46–49, 51.

Letter in "The Dark Triumvarite" by Jules Siegel. *Cavalier* (Aug. 1965): 14–16, 90.

"The World (This One), the Flesh (Mrs. Oedipa Maas), and the Testament of Pierce Inverarity." *Esquire* Dec. 1965: 170–73, 296, 298–303.

"A Gift of Books." *Holiday* 38, 6 (Dec. 1965): 164–65.

BIBLIOGRAPHY

"The Shrink Flips." *Cavalier* (March 1966): 32–33, 88–92.

"A Journey into the Mind of Watts." *New York Times Magazine* 12 June 1966: 34–35, 78, 80–82, 84.

"Pros and Cohns." Letter to the Editor, *New York Times Book Review* 17 July 1966: 22, 24.

"Pynchon Remembers Farina." *Cornell Alumni News* (June 1984): 20–23.

"Is It O.K. to Be a Luddite?" *New York Times Book Review* 28 Oct. 1984.

Selected Works About Pynchon

Bibliographies and Checklists

Clark, Beverly Lyon, and Caryn Fuoroli. "A Review of Major Pynchon Criticism." *Critical Essays on Thomas Pynchon.* Ed. Richard Pearce. Boston: G. K. Hall, 1981. 230–54. (Secondary)

Herzberg, Bruce. Bibliography. *Mindful Pleasures: Essays on Thomas Pynchon.* Ed. George Levine and David Leverenz. Boston: Little, Brown, 1976. 265–69. (Primary and Secondary)

_____. "Selected Articles on Thomas Pynchon: An Annotated Bibliography." *Twentieth Century Literature* 21 (1975): 221–25. (Secondary)

Scotto, Robert M. *Three Contemporary Novelists: An Annotated Bibliography of Works by and about John Hawkes, Joseph Heller, and Thomas Pynchon.* New York: Garland, 1977. (Primary and Secondary)

Walsh, Thomas P., and Cameron Northhouse. *John Barth, Jerzy Kosinski, and Thomas Pynchon: A Reference Guide.* Boston: G. K. Hall, 1977. (Primary and Secondary)

Weixlmann, Joseph. "Thomas Pynchon: A Bibliography." *Critique* 14, 2 (1972): 34–43. (Primary and Secondary)

BIBLIOGRAPHY

Books

Clerc, Charles, ed. *Approaches to Gravity's Rainbow*. Columbus: Ohio State University Press, 1982. Eight excellent essays study various aspects of the novel including war as a background, science and technology, psychological aspects, film, philosophical themes, language, and humor.

Cooper, Peter L. *Signs and Symptoms: Thomas Pynchon and the Contemporary World*. Berkeley: University of California Press, 1983. Besides establishing Pynchon's affinities with other counterrealists, Cooper works hard to demonstrate that Pynchon's thematic concerns emanate from contemporary political and social problems.

Cowart, David. *Thomas Pynchon: The Art of Allusion*. Carbondale: Southern Illinois University Press, 1980. Focuses on allusions to the arts in Pynchon's works, including the Remedios Varo painting in *Lot 49*, Puccini's *Manon Lescaut* in "Under the Rose" and *V.*, and *King Kong* in *Gravity's Rainbow*.

Fowler, Douglas. *A Reader's Guide to Gravity's Rainbow*. Ann Arbor: Ardis, 1980. Fowler insists that *Gravity's Rainbow* should be read as a poem. His book offers introductory sketches of major characters, motifs, and themes as well as a scene-by-scene guide to the novel.

Hite, Molly. *Idea of Order in the Novels of Thomas Pynchon*. Columbus: Ohio State University Press, 1983. Explores the teleological motivations behind Pynchon's novels while focusing on the tensions that are expressed through the polarities that inform his work.

Levine, George, and David Leverenz, eds. *Mindful Pleasures: Essays on Thomas Pynchon*. Boston: Little, Brown, 1976. Twelve of the most frequently cited essays in Pynchon scholarship.

Mackey, Douglas A. *The Rainbow Quest of Thomas Pynchon*.

142

BIBLIOGRAPHY

San Bernardino, CA: Borges Press, 1980. A brief and general introduction to the works.

Mendelson, Edward, ed. *Pynchon: A Collection of Critical Essays.* Englewood Cliffs, NJ: Prentice-Hall, 1978. Fourteen important essays, many of which focus on works before *Gravity's Rainbow,* and an illuminating introduction by the editor.

Pearce, Richard, ed. *Critical Essays on Thomas Pynchon.* Boston: G. K. Hall, 1981. Fourteen key essays on the novels and a review of major Pynchon criticism.

Plater, William M. *The Grim Phoenix: Reconstructing Thomas Pynchon.* Bloomington: Indiana University Press, 1978. Organized around themes rather than individual works, this study examines Pynchon's use of duality, the "tour," and the inanimate as means of perceiving reality.

Schaub, Thomas H. *Pynchon: The Voice of Ambiguity.* Urbana: University of Illinois Press, 1981. One of the best books to date on Pynchon, focusing on theories of reader response. Pays little attention to *V.,* but uses a compact analysis of *Lot 49* to extend into a complex investigation of *Gravity's Rainbow* that is particularly valuable concerning mandala imagery.

Siegel, Mark R. *Pynchon: Creative Paranoia in Gravity's Rainbow.* Port Washington, NY: Kennikat, 1978. An overview of *Gravity's Rainbow* that investigates the protean narrative voice as the primary vehicle for ambiguity and discusses filmic narrative technique, especially German expressionism.

Slade, Joseph W. *Thomas Pynchon.* New York: Warner, 1974. The first book-length study of Pynchon that offers a general introduction to the fiction.

Stark, John O. *Pynchon's Fictions: Thomas Pynchon and the Literature of Information.* Athens: Ohio University Press, 1980. Investigates the systems of information—psychology, history, religion, and science—that play roles in organizing Pynchon's fictional worlds while emphasizing Pynchon's

BIBLIOGRAPHY

recognition that all theories and systems are themselves
ultimately fictions.

Tanner, Tony. *Thomas Pynchon.* New York and London:
Methuen, 1982. A brief but brilliant overview of Pynchon's
work with a chapter devoted to the short fiction and one each
to the novels.

Selected Articles and Parts of Books

Berressem, Hanjo. "Godolphin-Goodolphin-Goodol'phin-Good
ol'Pyn-Good ol'Pym: A Question of Integration." *Pynchon
Notes* 10 (Oct. 1982): 3–17. Explores Pynchon's use of Poe's *The
Narrative of Arthur Gordon Pym* in *V.*

Fussell, Paul. *The Great War and Modern Memory.* New York:
Oxford University Press, 1975. 328–34. Includes a discussion of
historical prototypes for The White Visitation in *Gravity's
Rainbow.*

Henkle, Roger B. "Pynchon's Tapestries on the Western Wall."
Modern Fiction Studies 17, 2 (1971): 207–20. Examines *V.* and
Lot 49 in terms of historical and literary antecedents while
pointing out flaws in Pynchon's characterization. One of the
standard essays on Pynchon's early novels.

Leland, John P. "Pynchon's Linguistic Demon: *The Crying of Lot
49.*" *Critique* 16, 2 (1974): 45–53. Uses Maxwell's Demon as a
metaphor to discuss the exploration of the possbilities of
language in *Lot 49.*

Leverenz, David. "On Trying to Read *Gravity's Rainbow.*"
Mindful Pleasures: Essays on Thomas Pynchon. Ed. George
Levine and David Leverenz. Boston: Little, Brown, 1976. 229–
49. Discusses major patterns through which the reader may
attempt to make sense of *Gravity's Rainbow.*

Lhamon, W. T., Jr. "Pentecost, Promiscuity, and Pynchon's *V.*:
From the Scaffold to the Impulsive." *Twentieth Century
Literature* 21, 2 (1975): 163–75. Investigates religious imagery
in *V.*, particularly references to the Paraclete.

BIBLIOGRAPHY

MacAdam, Alfred. "Pynchon as Satirist: To Write, to Mean." *Yale Review* 67 (1975): 555–66. Shows how Pynchon appropriates one of the principal plots of the romance, the quest, and uses it for satiric purposes.

McConnell, Frank. D. *Four Postwar American Novelists: Bellow, Mailer, Barth, Pynchon.* Chicago: University of Chicago Press, 1977. 159–97. The section on Pynchon contributes a brief but penetrating overview of the three novels while aligning Pynchon with major trends in contemporary American fiction.

Mangel, Anne. "Maxwell's Demon, Entropy, Information: *The Crying of Lot 49.*" *TriQuarterly* 20 (1971): 194–208. Seminal essay on Pynchon's treatment of entropy in *Lot 49.*

Mendelson, Edward. "Gravity's Encyclopedia." *Mindful Pleasures: Essays on Thomas Pynchon.* Ed. George Levine and David Leverenz. Boston: Little, Brown, 1976. 161–95. One of the most important essays on *Gravity's Rainbow,* in which Mendelson places it within the genre of encyclopedic narrative. He traces Pynchon's indebtedness to Max Weber and shows Pynchon's concern with the political implications of language.

Newman, Robert D. "Pynchon's Use of Carob in *V.*" *Notes on Contemporary American Literature* 9, 3 (1981): 11. The relation of carob to Fausto Maijstral's role as a John the Baptist figure.

_____. "The White Goddess Restored: Affirmation in Pynchon's *V.*" *University of Mississippi Studies in English* 4 (1983): 178–86. Demonstrates Paola Maijstral's role as an affirmative White Goddess figure who functions in opposition to the destructive force of V.

Poirier, Richard. "The Importance of Thomas Pynchon." *Twentieth Century Literature* 21, 2 (1975): 151–62. Poirier argues that *Gravity's Rainbow* should be ranked with *Ulysses* and *Moby-Dick* while justifying Pynchon's place as a major writer.

BIBLIOGRAPHY

_____. "Rocket Power." *Saturday Review of the Arts* 1, 3 (1973): 59–64. Perhaps the most eloquent and intelligent early review of *Gravity's Rainbow.*

Richardson, Robert O. "The Absurd Animate in Thomas Pynchon's *V.*" *Studies in the Twentieth Century* 9 (1972): 35–58. Discusses positive characters in *V.*—Rachel, Paola, and Fausto—who counter the generally entropic emphasis in the novel.

Sanders, Scott. "Pynchon's Paranoid History." *Twentieth Century Literature* 21, 2 (1975): 177–92. Examines extensions of the Puritan imagination within the secular world as portrayed in the paranoid patterns in *Gravity's Rainbow.*

Schaub, Thomas H. "Where Have We Been, Where Are We Headed? A Retrospective View of Pynchon Criticism." *Pynchon Notes* 7 (Oct. 1983): 5–21. Review of the trends in Pynchon criticism.

Seed, David. "Fantasy and Dream in Thomas Pynchon's 'Low-lands.'" *Rocky Mountain Review* 37, 1–2 (1983): 54–68. Along with Slade's discussion of references to "The Waste Land" in his book, this is the best explication of "Low-lands."

_____. "Order in Thomas Pynchon's 'Entropy.'" *Journal of Narrative Technique* 11 (1981): 135–53. Excellent discussion of the dual meanings of entropy as an organizing function in the story.

Siegel, Jules. "Who Is Thomas Pynchon . . . and Why Did He Take Off with My Wife." *Playboy* Mar. 1977: 97. Offers some biographical insights. The reliability of the author is, however, questionable.

Simberloff, Daniel. "Entropy, Information and Life: Biophysics in the Novels of Thomas Pynchon." *Perspectives in Biology and Medicine* 21 (1978): 617. One of several articles explicating scientific allusions in Pynchon's novels.

Slade, Joseph W. "Religion, Psychology, Sex, and Love in

BIBLIOGRAPHY

Gravity's Rainbow." Approaches to Gravity's Rainbow. Ed. Charles Clerc. Columbus: Ohio State University Press, 1982. 153–98. An immensely informative essay that discusses the influences of Weber, Calvinism, Eliot, Brown, Jung, and Marcuse.

Tanner, Tony. City of Words: American Fiction, 1950–1970. New York: Harper and Row, 1971. 153–80. The chapter entitled "Caries and Cabals" offers extensive readings of V. and Lot 49. A standard in Pynchon criticism, the essay views Pynchon's fiction as an investigation into the necessity of establishing patterns of explanation to account for a chaotic world.

Winston, Mathew. "The Quest for Pynchon." Twentieth Century Literature 21, 3 (1975): 278–87. The best biographical essay on Pynchon to date.

Wofley, Lawrence C. "Repression's Rainbow: The Presence of Norman O. Brown in Pynchon's Big Novel." PMLA 92 (1978): 873–79. A key article to understanding the thematic dimensions of Gravity's Rainbow. Investigates the influence of Brown's Life Against Death, particularly the application of Freudian concepts of repression and sublimation to the process of culture formation.

Young, James Dean. "The Enigma Variations of Thomas Pynchon." Critique 10, 1 (1967): 69–77. Early essay that examines V. and Lot 49 through Pynchon's foiling of traditional expectations regarding character, history, and geography.

Journal

Pynchon Notes, edited by Khachig Tölöyan, has appeared since October 1979. It publishes essays on all aspects of Pynchon's work, contains reviews of books dealing with Pynchon's work, and includes a current bibliography in each issue. It is published twice a year, in the spring and fall, and is obtainable from the English Department, Wesleyan University, Middletown, CT 06457.

INDEX

INDEX

INDEX

INDEX

INDEX

INDEX

INDEX

INDEX

PACIFIC UNIVERSITY LIBRARY
FOREST GROVE, OREGON